D0842971

Quality 50 ≌

by Les Line, Editor of Audubon magazine, and Ann and Myron Sutton

A Chanticleer Press Edition

THE AUDUBON SOCIETY
BOOK OF TREES

HARRY N. ABRAMS, INC., PUBLISHERS, NEW YORK

For Michael and Heather; may they always have forests to explore.

Library of Congress Cataloging in Publication Data
Line, Les
The Audubon Society book of trees
"A Chanticleer Press edition."
Includes Index.
1. Trees. I. Sutton, Ann, 1923-   joint author. II. Sutton, Myron, joint
author. III. National Audubon Society. IV. Title. OK 475.L5 1981 582.13
81-781 ISBN 0-8109-0673-2 AACR2
Published in 1981 by Harry N. Abrams, Incorporated, New York

Prepared and produced by Chanticleer Press, Inc.
Manufactured in Japan.

Chanticleer Staff:
Publisher: Paul Steiner
Editor-in-Chief: Milton Rugoff
Managing Editor: Gudrun Buettner
Project Editor: Mary Suffudy
Assistant Editor: Ann Hodgman
Production: Helga Lose, Dean Gibson
Art Associates: Carol Nehring, Mary Gregory deButts
Picture Library: Joan Lynch, Edward Douglas
Design: Massimo Vignelli

*Note on Illustration Numbers: All illustrations are numbered according
to the pages on which they appear.*

Excerpt from *The Wonderful Adventures of Paul Bunyan,* courtesy of
The Heritage Press, Norwalk, Connecticut.

First frontispiece: *A yucca grows in the crotch of an ancient live oak*
(Quercus virginiana) *on Cumberland Island, Georgia.* (James P. Valentine/
Quest Foundation)

Second frontispiece: *A twisted vine maple* (Acer circinatum) *is covered
with moss in Redwood National Park, California.* (Harald Sund)

Third frontispiece: *A maple* (Acer sp.) *blazes in full autumn color in the
Jordan River Valley of Michigan.* (John Shaw)

Fourth frontispiece: *Autumn comes to the valley of the Allagash River,
in Maine, where birches* (Betula sp.) *flash their characteristic golden
hues.* (Charles Steinhacker)

Fifth frontispiece: *A fresh snowfall decorates Douglas-fir* (Pseudotsuga
menziesii) *and western hemlock* (Tsuga heterophylla) *on Vancouver
Island, British Columbia.* (Steven C. Wilson/Entheos)

Contents

Fifty years from now, a book of this beauty and magnitude might be impossible to assemble. For the forests of the world, and the wondrous life-forms they sustain, are disappearing at a rate that frightens ecologists and conservationists. Reports *Newsweek* magazine:

"By ax, bulldozer, chain saw, and fire, the world's trees are falling—far faster than nature or man can replace them. Up to half the world's woodlands may have vanished since 1950, and annual losses now are running between 1 and 2 percent—25 to 50 million acres."

An environmental expert at the U.S. State Department puts those figures into perspective: "It is safe to say that a country the size of Cuba is being destroyed each year. At that rate, the very existence of the tropical forests is being called into question."

"A grim, some say unstoppable, war on trees" is how *Newsweek* describes the assault on the great equatorial green belt. "Two-thirds of Latin America's original forest is gone or seriously depleted. Half of Africa's woodlands has disappeared. Thailand has lost one-quarter of its forest in the last ten years, and the Philippines, one-seventh in the last five. Spreading patches of the Amazon, Central Africa, and the Himalayan foothills have taken on the moonscape look of North Africa and the Middle East—both of which once boasted verdant stands of trees."

The war on trees is not, however, confined to the tropical forests. A recent report by the Worldwatch Institute suggests that wood could provide up to one-fifth of America's energy by the end of this century. The forecasters are talking not so much about hand-split cords of hardwood burned in cast-iron stoves as about 50-megawatt wood-fired powerplants—huge generating facilities fed by great machines that digest entire trees, entire forests, from their topmost leaves to the roots and spew out endless tons of chips for the boilers.

The war on trees takes many forms. The forests of Southeast Asia are being ravaged for their valuable hardwood by giant multinational corporations; by 1990, for instance, loggers will have totally denuded the lowland forests of Malaysia and the Philippines. In Central America, forests are being converted to pastureland to provide cheap hamburger for fast-food restaurants in the United States. In the Amazon Basin, the richest man in America is stripping and burning the native rain forest from an area larger than the state of Connecticut; his 5,800-square-mile holdings are to be replanted with fast-growing exotic trees that are expected to yield both timber and paper. In Africa, the annual loss of prime forests totals more than 4 million acres a year; most of the wood is burned as fuel by poverty-stricken natives.

The war on trees also has many consequences: erosion, flood, famine, the spread of deserts. The Amazon, for instance, has been called "a counterfeit paradise." It isn't the soil that is fertile, but the lush foliage. At least 70 percent of the total nutrient supply of the tropical forest is found in the living biomass. "The soil's main function is to support, not nourish," wrote ecologist Anne LaBastille. "Most of Amazonia is a desert covered with trees." Thus schemes for large-scale exploitation of the Amazon for agriculture and growing so-called supertrees seem doomed to failure—at grievous environmental costs.

Not the least of those costs is the impoverishment of Earth's flora and fauna. The tropical rain forests in particular support an incredibly diverse population of plant and animal species. Whereas Great Britain has 1,430 native plant species, the Malay Peninsula— half its size—boasts 7,900 kinds of plants. One out of every five birds on our planet evolved in Amazonia. And on a 100-acre plot near Manaus, Brazil, 235 species of trees were identified; an area of similar size in New England might contain 10 different trees. Tropical forests have given man such life-saving drugs as quinine, and such important food staples as bananas and pineapples. But at the present rate of forest destruction, it is estimated that one million species of plants and animals will become extinct by the year 2000. Their biological, economic, and cultural values will never be catalogued.

I am grateful that my job, as editor of *Audubon*, has enabled me to visit many of the world's great forest ecosystems—from the tundra of Alaska to the rain-drenched mountains of Costa Rica, from the mangrove mazes of the Florida Everglades to the saguaro deserts of Arizona. I am grateful, too, that Paul Steiner asked me to participate in this magnificent book, fifth in the series sponsored by the National Audubon Society. For its pages clearly show what we stand to lose if a truce is not declared in our war on trees.

THE AUDUBON SOCIETY BOOK OF TREES

16. *A small tree of hammocks and rocky shores from southern Florida to the West Indies and Belize, Florida thatch palm (Thrinax radiata) has fan-shaped leaves nearly 4 feet in diameter. Worldwide, there are some 2,800 species of palms in tropical and subtropical regions; they range from woody vines to towering trees with unbranched, columnar trunks. Many palms are important economically, producing coconuts, dates, copra, oil, wax, fibers, and thatch to cover roofs.* (Walter H. Hodge)

Shadows of Life and Death: The Tropical Forest

Beyond the Carrao River in southeastern Venezuela one reaches about as far from modern civilization as possible among the shadowed mysteries of the Orinoco River basin. Travelers land at an airstrip more than 1,000 miles beyond Ciudad Bolívar, one of the farthest outposts. From the airstrip scarcely even a trail leads into the wilderness. Travel is by canoe. Or overland across the savanna. Or behind an Indian guide who knows of openings through the forest or cuts them with a *penilla*. But there is something special about this forest. In five days on the river—if we survive—we shall reach a remarkable destination. And pass through one of the most complex forest ecosystems on earth.

Our canoe glides over the waters as over a mirror. The river is dyed with brown organic matter that makes it seem as though we are paddling in coffee. We feel at first a pervasive sense of unease and cannot decipher the sounds we hear, or see what flits in the underbrush and vanishes. Through trees that border the river we glimpse a broad savanna and then a knoll. Far off, out of the jungle, rises a towering table mountain called a *tepui*, remnant of the Guayana Shield—a continental mass of red sandstone that has been eroding for millions of years.

We must have flown over a hundred million trees to get here, trees so densely packed that nothing is visible beneath them. Nothing breaks their continuity except an occasional glint of sunlight reflected from hidden waterways. Before the first day ends we have been struck by a singular recognition: here is not one tropical forest but a hundred, and not one principal tree but a thousand.

The night air hardly cools the woods and next day we experience again the high humidity and temperatures on which this vegetation thrives. Trees of all descriptions, massed in a wall, come to the river's edge. Some dip their branches into the water. Palms grow out of the river itself. Branches and leaves, fallen and broken off upstream, float on the water surface.

We search for the *Tabebuia*, though how hopeless it is to seek one tree among so many. We shall know it at blooming time, when *Tabebuias* lose their leaves and the flowers may be seen for miles in a dazzling display. *Tabebuias* in Puerto Rico lift a blaze of orange or crimson into the misty air. In Costa Rica they gleam with a sulfur yellow. The *Tabebuia ipe*, national tree of Paraguay, may reach 125 feet in height and 6 feet in diameter—a huge bulk imperiously strung with rose-pink blossoms.

Jacaranda is also here. And every tropical forest seems to have wild figs. The strangler fig (*Ficus*), a tree with wide-spreading branches, frequently seeds itself in the tops of other trees. From there it drops long roots to the ground, enclosing and stifling the host tree. The famed banyan tree (*F. benghalensis*) of India is a fig; so is the "rubber" plant (*F. elastica*), a familiar potted ornamental.

As the river narrows we feel enclosed by a ragged line of dense forest. Trees even cling to the faces of gray cliffs that rise for thousands of feet up into the clouds. Everywhere that roots can grip the stone or soil and receive abundant water the tropical forest thrives. Rainfall in the lowlands measures from 70 to 160 inches a year. Temperatures vary as little as two degrees from season to season. In such a stable environment, trees may exceed 100 feet in height, though for the most part they remain slender. In all Venezuela, botanists have identified 40,000 species of plants and are convinced that there are living trees as yet undiscovered. Here in the Orinoco Basin hundreds of plant species are endemic—growing here and nowhere else. Venezuelans call the vegetation *exuberante*. The weight of all these trees, called the standing biomass, has been estimated to exceed 400,000 pounds per acre at any given time. That richness attests to the flow of minerals, scant though it may seem in impoverished sandy soil, and the ability of trees to extract these minerals for survival.

And atop the *tepuis*—those tablelands so conspicuous on nearly every horizon? We see the rims of their summits from the river, and we would scale the walls only with supreme difficulty. But from aircraft skimming the summits we look down upon gigantic naked rocks surrounded by patches of trees reduced by the cooler climate to less than 30 feet in height.

By the third day of working our way upstream it has become clear that nature knew no limit here. "The most important single characteristic of the Tropical Rain Forest," wrote the British scientist P. W. Richards, "is its astonishing wealth of species." We have seen so much we cannot resist the question: how many species of trees are there? Alexander von Humboldt, the German naturalist, who explored the Orinoco River in 1800, had much the same question: "The excessive diversity of the flora and its richness in flowering plants forbids one to ask 'What is the composition of these forests?'" Venezuelan biologists today answer simply: *"Cómo sabemos?"* How can we tell? Less than 2 percent of the region has been explored scientifically. But they point to one of the *tepuis,* rising massively from the lowland forest, and say: "We have discovered 826 species of plants on Auyantepui. It is only a beginning." In another tropical forest of Venezuela, an estimated 600 species of plants have been identified on one hectare (2.471 acres).

In our passage upstream we come to Orchid Island, known for its abundance of epiphytes, and a reminder of the more than a thousand species of orchids growing in this region, not the least of which is the magnificent *Cattleya superba*.

A parrot screams from the tall trees and then flies overhead in a flash of green and red. Yet wild animals are less often seen here than in other forest ecosystems because they are shy or secluded. In some tropical forests, tapirs and jaguars may be encountered, but only rarely. Such animals are more prevalent toward the open savannas. The exception, of course, is an immense population of insects, which swarm at all levels of the tropical forest. Many of these are brilliantly colored, such as the gala bug and certain butterflies.

One prominent mammal, however, does live in this

forest. Through curtains of rattan, in the green caverns of the forest, slip the naked, agile Yanomamö, native human beings whose lives and culture differ markedly from those of people in the industrialized world. They are adapted to the world of trees and rivers about them. Their tools are wood and bone. Their jewelry consists of flowers, feathers, and seeds. From soot and resin mixed with pigments they make paints. For food they have bananas, pineapples, dates, worms, ants, spiders, lizards, snakes, owls. They make boats from *Bursera* wood. Unlike other primitive peoples who adopted civilized ways only to suffer disease and starvation, these retain their hunting skills and life of abundance.

As we float along in a leafy sea it seems difficult to imagine conifers here, but botanists have discovered at least four species of *Podocarpus*, resident in nearly all rain forests. Among hundreds of other trees are *Cordia*, *Clusia*, and moriche palms (*Mauritia flexuosa*). None dominates. All seem fused in an amorphous tidal wave of green.

We turn up a side stream in a tree-filled gorge, and after five days on the river reach our destination. Through the foliage we at last glimpse what we came to see, one of the world's greatest wonders: a series of cascades issuing from openings near the top of the cliff and plunging 3,000 feet past tree-lined ledges into the woods below. It is Angel Falls, highest on earth. Unless, of course, somewhere lost in another valley hides a waterfall that is even higher.

It could be. There are millions of acres left to explore, all set aside as Canaima National Park, one of the largest natural reserves in South America. The British author W. H. Hudson called these Venezuelan forests *Green Mansions*, a name he gave to his most famous novel. In truth, there are green mansions, with numerous shared characteristics, through much of the rest of Latin America, West Africa, Southeast Asia, Australia, and islands in the sea. There are also cloud forests, where the tropical woods rise to high elevations and are soaked in mists. They produce fewer wild animals but the vegetative communities are rich in trees, orchids, and other epiphytes. Higher yet, the forests diminish in size and extent. At elevations of 19,000 feet they are no more, replaced by jagged peaks and perpetual ice.

21. *In the rain forest of Costa Rica, a stream tumbles over a series of ledges into a deep, cool pool. Such scenes may soon be found only in a handful of national parks, for the world's tropical forests are being destroyed at a rate that frightens ecologists. In Central America alone, two-thirds of the original forest has been devastated and another 2.5 million acres is denuded annually. Half of the world's plant and animal species are found in tropical forests, and scientists warn that fully 20 percent could become extinct by the year 2000.* (John Shaw)

22 *overleaf. It is the dry season on the Gran Sabana of Venezuela, and a silk-cotton tree (Ceiba pentandra) in full pink flower towers over the savanna forest canopy. These massive deciduous trees have trunks 8 feet in diameter; their first branches may be 100 feet above the ground, and the crown will spread for 150 feet. Silk-cotton trees occur not in groups but scattered throughout the tropical forest. They flower simultaneously, greatly increasing the chance for cross-pollination.* (Edward S. Ross)

*24 and **25.** The many wonderful
and beautiful orchids found in the
Costa Rica rain forest include*
Brassavola digbyana *(24) and*
Epidendrum pseudepidendrum *(25).
Some 10 percent of the world's
flowering plants belong to the
Orchidacea, the largest of all plant
families. Some 20,000 species of
orchids have been described, but
botanists believe many more await
discovery. Given the rapid destruction of tropical forests, many
orchids may be obliterated before
they are even catalogued. Like
these two species, most orchids
grow as epiphytes on the trunks
and branches of tropical trees.*
Epidendrum pseudepidendrum *has
a flamelike lip that attracts*

pollinating hummingbirds.
(24 Kjell B. Sandved/N.A.S./Photo
Researchers, Inc.; 25 James H.
Carmichael, Jr./N.A.S./Photo
Researchers, Inc.)

26 *and* **27.** *Although native orchids were cultivated in China in the 28th century before Christ, it was 1698 before the first tropical orchid—a specimen from Curacao in the West Indies—reached Europe. Another century passed before an orchid-collecting mania was triggered in England by the arrival from Brazil of the first plants of the genus* Cattleya. *Soon expeditions were being dispatched to tropical forests to fetch thousands of orchids for auctions in Liverpool and London, where a particularly rare plant would bring £1,000. One team, invading the jungles of Colombia in the 1890s, felled 4,000 trees to gather 10,000 orchid plants.* Cattleya bowringiana

(26), native to Honduras, belongs to a genus that has produced the large, ruffled orchids most often worn on festive occasions. Epidendrum radicans *(27) is a fairly common orchid found from Mexico to northern South America. It is a lithophyte, growing on rock outcroppings in open areas.* (26 Hans D. Dossenbach; 27 John Shaw)

28 *overleaf. In the rainy season, African tuliptree (*Spathodea campanulata*) unveils cup-shaped, orange-scarlet flowers nearly 5 inches long. The flower buds secrete so much water that this evergreen tree, native to West Africa but planted throughout the tropics as an ornamental, is called the "fountain tree."* (Walter H. Hodge)

32 *overleaf. Large, umbrellalike leaves identify a cecropia tree in a misty Costa Rica rain forest. Some 100 species of tropical trees belong to this New World genus. All have hollow stems inhabited by fierce ants that live in a symbiotic relationship with the host trees. The cecropias provide the ants with food and shelter; in turn, they defend the trees against attacks by leaf-cutting insects. Cecropias yield a milky sap used for medicines by natives; and the hollow stems are often made into musical instruments; the leaves are the favored food of sloths.* (John Shaw)

30 *and* **31.** *The cannonball tree* (Couroupita guianensis) *of the lowland rainforest of the Guianas produces its unusual, fragrant flowers on tangled woody stalks that emerge directly from the trunk. Bats pollinate the 5-inch-wide blossoms. The fruit, ripening over a period of 18 months, is truly a "cannonball," hard-shelled and nearly 8 inches in diameter.* (Walter H. Hodge)

35. *Developing stems of giant bamboo* (Dendrocalamus giganteus) *of Burma may grow 15 inches in a day, soon reaching a mature height of 120 feet. Few natural materials can claim the incredible versatility of bamboo; among its hundreds of uses over the centuries are the making of bridges, ships, houses, aqueducts, weapons of war, and paper. Young bamboo shoots are used in gourmet cooking. And such rare animals as the mountain gorilla of Congo forests and the giant panda of China depend on bamboo foliage for food.* (Walter H. Hodge)

34. *A closeup of the culm, or hollow stem, of common bamboo* (Bambusa vulgaris). *Bamboos belong to the huge grass family Gramineae, and thus are relatives of corn, wheat, and other important grains. But the classification of bamboos is something of a puzzle for botanists, who place the number of species worldwide at anywhere from 500 to 1,000. Tropical* Bambusa vulgaris *has been so widely planted that experts cannot trace its origin. Pieces of its under-ground stems, or rhizomes, are commonly planted in crop fields to produce fast-growing supports for climbing plants such as beans.* (Walter H. Hodge)

36. *Leaves of an epiphytic filmy fern* (Trichomanes tuerckheimii) *cling to a tree trunk in the wet Amazon forest. The 500 or more kinds of filmy ferns, with delicate, semi-transparent leaves only one cell thick, are largely epiphytes of the dark, wet rainforests of the tropics. The graceful leaves of most filmy ferns are usually pendant, but in* Trichomanes tuerckheimii, *they are appressed tightly to the bark, which they grasp with prehensile, rust-colored hairs.* (Kjell B. Sandved)

37. *Fungi are vital components of the tropical forest ecosystem, decomposing dead wood and the steady rain of leaves, flowers, and twigs from trees far above. Their work is done so quickly that a fallen leaf virtually disappears in two or three months. Some cosmopolitan fungi, such as* Polyporus versicolor *(37 top)* and P. cinnabarinus *(37 bottom) seen here growing in the Amazon basin, are large and colorful. But most survive unnoticed in the forest litter and soil. All are saprophytes, devoid of chlorophyll and thus obtaining their nourishment by converting plant tissues to simple foods like sugar.*
(Loren McIntyre)

38 *overleaf. The leopard* (Panthera pardus) *is a powerful, solitary hunter of African and Asian forests. Standing 2½ feet at the shoulders and weighing 180 pounds, it kills from ambush, then carries its prey into the branches to keep it safe from scavengers. Leopards hunt deer, antelope, primates, and a wide variety of birds.*
(Stanley Breeden)

40. *A three-toed sloth* (Bradypus sp.) *climbs a cecropia tree in the Amazon jungle. The rain forests of tropical America are home to the world's 7 species of sloths, who rarely use their long powerful claws for defense. For they have thick, loose skin and can roll themselves into tight balls for protection. Also, green algae on their dense fur offers a measure of camouflage in this largely green world.* (Wolfgang Bayer)

41 *top left. A female silver langur* (Presbytis cristatus) *cuddles her infant in the Java jungle. One of 14 species of langurs—Asiatic monkeys whose principal diet is leaves—the silver langur lives a totally arboreal life, and may never descend to the ground.* (Tom McHugh/N.A.S./Photo Researchers, Inc.)

41 *top right. Of all New World monkeys, only uakaris have short tails—about 5½ inches long, compared with the 12-inch appendage of the little squirrel monkey and the 29-inch tail of spider monkeys. Inhabitants of riverbottom forests, uakaris are able to run on two legs, using their arms for balance. Moving quietly through the treetops, the red-faced uakari* (Cacajao rubicundus) *eats fruit, flowers, and insects.* (Robert C. Hermes/N.A.S./Photo Researchers, Inc.)

41 *above. From the vantage point of a palm frond, squirrel monkeys* (Saimiri sciurea) *survey their domain—a small island in the Amazon River. This is the most common monkey in South America, living in troops that contain a hundred or more individuals. The squirrel monkey's varied diet includes insects, crabs, snails, and tree frogs.* (Loren McIntyre)

42 *and* **43.** *Tropical forests are a lepidopterist's dream world, for the variety and beauty of their moth and butterfly populations seems unlimited. From Queensland, Australia, come Ornithoptera priamus (42 top) a stunning birdwing butterfly with wings 7 inches across, and Papilio ulysses (42 bottom), a somewhat smaller swallowtail butterfly. As was so often the case, early lepidopterists named both species for heroes of Greek mythology—Ulysses and King Priam. Freshly emerged from their crysallides in the rain forests of Australia are red lacewing butterflies (Cethosia chrysippe, 43). Most famous of all tropical forest butterflies are the morphoes of South America, whose iridescent blue wings can even be spotted by pilots flying over the trackless forests. (Belinda Wright)*

46 *overleaf. A pair of scarlet macaws* (Ara macao) *flash through the canopy of the Amazon forest. Macaws not only are the largest of all parrots, averaging 40 inches in length; they are among the most brilliantly colored. Their plumage often consists of sharply defined patches of solid colors—red or green—abutting gold or blue. The huge and powerful macaw bill is used for climbing about treetops and crushing nuts and fruits. Their numbers decimated by the pet trade, wild macaws have become an uncommon sight in the New World tropics.* (Loren McIntyre)

44 *and* **45.** *Among the smaller inhabitants of tropical American rain forests are* Dendrobates pumilio *(44), one of the arrow-poison frogs, and* Hyla leucophyllata *(45), a beautifully marked tree frog. Indians will pierce an arrow-poison frog with a stick and hold it above a fire, causing poison to drip from the animal's sweat glands. Arrows are then dipped in the poison, which instantly paralyzes monkeys and birds.* Hyla leuco-phyllata *is found from the Amazon Basin to the Guianas. Its voice suggests a very large cricket, and if handled the frog gives off an odor like that of nasturtium leaves.* (44 John Shaw; 45 Joseph T. Collins/ N.A.S./Photo Researchers, Inc.)

48. *A silk-cotton tree* (Ceiba pentandra) *on the West African plain. Though native to the New World tropics, this tree has been widely planted in Asia, Africa, and the Philippines for its yield of kapok—a mass of floss that fills seed pods up to six inches long. Lightweight and impervious to water, kapok is used to stuff life preservers, furniture, and pillows.* (Kjell B. Sandved)

Wide-open Spaces: Parklands and Savannas

In sharp contrast to humid, densely packed tropical rain forests are trees in the open. In addition to being less crowded, a tree has another advantage in growing apart from its neighbors—it does not compete with other members of the grove for sunlight, water, and minerals. But there are disadvantages. The lone tree is more vulnerable to wind, heat, cold, and drought. It may also be surrounded by tall grasses, a very great danger when those grasses dry out and lightning or human carelessness sends great sheets of flame across the landscape.

Such is the perilous life of trees on savannas. The term "savanna" has various meanings; the simplest defines it as an area of grass and trees. At one extreme, where there are fewer trees, the region approaches grassland. At the other, the number of trees increases to what we call a woodland or parkland—open forest and grassy glades. Nature spaces the trees in what seems like a random manner, but, as always, controls the distribution of the members of the community, except, of course, where savannas have been burned, farmed, grazed, or logged by man. Hanno, the Carthaginian explorer, reported grass-burning by the inhabitants of Africa prior to 480 B.C.

Savannas may be wet or dry, densely or sparsely forested; sometimes they are named for their principal tree species, such as palm savanna. They may be high or low in elevation. They are not limited to interior locations: coastal savannas are common in the tropics and subtropics.

One factor common to all is a distinct dry season or two each year. Some places are flooded for six months and arid for six months. Few but hardy or versatile trees can survive such an alteration of feast and famine. The grass on some savannas, as in lowland Nepal, is drenched by monsoon rains and grows "higher than an elephant's eye." Any young tree trying to grow up through such thick grass has to be vigorous and adaptable. For when the monsoon ends, the grass dries out, and one can imagine the roar and heat when wind-fanned flames leap 30 feet or more into the air. Trees in their path cannot fly away like locusts. Either they can withstand the heat or they are reduced to ashes.

Africa has some of the largest of the world's savannas. One north of the equatorial forests stretches between Dakar and the Nile River—a distance of more than 3,000 miles. The principal trees there are *Isoberlinia*, one of several types of trees whose seed pods explode when ripe. Another savanna sweeps from coast to coast across the waist of Africa, south of the equatorial rain forests. This region, abounding in trees, is known as miombo woodland. It is the dominant natural habitat in Zambia's Kafue National Park, which covers 5,600,000 acres. Leaves drop during droughts, adding to the flammable material, and fire blackens the landscape periodically. But when the leaves grow back as a new rainy season begins, they produce a brilliant red-copper-bronze-green succession of colors much as do certain eucalyptus trees in Australia. In a woodland composed of *Brachystegia longifolia*, *B. speciformis*, and *Julbernadia paniculata*, this kaleidoscope of colors in the African miombo heralds the beginning of spring.

Greater kudu, sable antelope, hartebeest, kob, puku, and zebra, even the yellow baboon, inhabit these woodlands. Survival can be a matter of chance; even though savanna grasses look nutritious, some haven't much protein and are no more palatable than wire mesh. Favorite haunts of elephants are forests of large mopane trees (*Colophospermum mopane*), which grow here and there in the miombo and become dominant to the south.

One animal, literally above all others, has become adapted to feeding in trees without having to climb them. The giraffe finds savanna woodlands ideal habitat in which to roam without tangling its long neck in a mass of interlocking branches. Having little competition in gathering leaves as much as 18 feet above the ground, it doesn't have to travel far in search of food. In a stand of whistling thorns (*Acacia drepanolobium*), which have thousands of treacherous spikes, we wonder how any animal that feeds there can avoid impaling itself. But with its long, prehensile, sticky tongue the giraffe is able to grasp selected bunches of leaves. And if that becomes too difficult, the animal dines on young tips of branches where thorns are soft.

In the giraffe's long evolution, many forests have diminished temporarily or begun to die out, leaving a few trees standing by themselves. Thus the mvule tree (*Chlorophora excelsa*), which now is isolated out on grasslands, is a survivor of ancient forests cut back by fire. Perhaps the original forest was opened by marauding elephants and thus made more vulnerable to burning. Given a few years without fires, however, more trees may rise up, shade out the grasses, and reestablish a woodland.

Savannas differ greatly not only in Africa but around the world. Those of the Ivory Coast are dominated by a palm, *Borassus aethiopum*, but other species grow there: *Crossopterix febrifuga*, *Piliostigma thonningii*, *Bridelia ferruginea*, and *Cussonia barteri*. The savannas of southern Asia resemble those of Africa, at least superficially. The grasses include *Andropogon*, *Polytoea*, and *Themeda*, and among the trees we encounter spiny acacias (*Acacia tomentosa*), jujube trees (*Zizyphus jujuba*), and gebang palms (*Corypha utan*). Bright color is often characteristic. One of those species that blooms while leafless, the *Erythrina* or coral tree, displays bold red flowers. A closely related species on African savannas, *Erythrina senegalensis*, has scarlet flowers and scarlet seeds. On Asian savannas the tamarind (*Tamarindus indicus*) and *Sterculia foetida* are important food trees for animals.

The temperate latitudes also have their savannas. Spain is known for extensive woodlands of evergreen oak (*Quercus ilex*), which is also found around the Mediterranean Sea to the Middle East.

The huge savannas of Brazil have abundant rainfall— 40 to 70 inches annually—but also, typically, a long and severe drought every year. On South American savannas the grasses, especially *Paspalum*, seem tougher and more rigid than those on other continents. One unusual tree set apart on Brazilian and Argentine savannas is the picturesque *Araucaria*, among the most ancient of conifers. Stiff, sharp-pointed leaves offer a challenge to any animal trying to ascend it.

Savannas have developed across large areas of Colombia and Venezuela. In the Orinoco River basin a white sandy topsoil overlies an impermeable red clay, but *Curatella americana* and other trees do well among the short bunchgrass (*Tragopogon*). On Bolivian savannas the most common trees are *Tabebuia suberosa*, *Curatella americana*, and a palm, *Copernicia cerifera*.

As for Australia, the ghost gum (*Eucalyptus papuana*) exists on savannas over the northern part of the continent. Woollybutt (*E. miniata*) and Darwin stringybark (*E. tetrodonta*) thrive in savanna woodlands, but only because they are able to live with the absence of rain from April to December.

The South Florida slash pine (*Pinus elliotti* var. *densa*) does well on limestone flats and ridges, presiding over an understory of saw grass (*Cladium*) or saw palmetto (*Serenoa repens*), but it has to endure dry seasons and the assault of fire sweeping in from the Everglades. Its bark has insulative properties that form something of a fireproof forest; it is able to make a comeback after being charred.

One of the best-known parkland species in North America is ponderosa pine (*Pinus ponderosa*), a huge, handsome orange-trunked tree that in parts of its range survives two distinct dry seasons of three months each, one beginning in April and another in October. The individuals of this species are usually well spaced, once a grove of them matures; hence the pronounced parkland aspect. Typically, herds of elk and mule deer circulate among the pines, bears climb into them, squirrels nest, tanagers sing, dark-crested Steller's jays fly rowdily from one tree to another, and sunsets turn the trunks a flaming red.

53. *A giant baobab* (Adansonia digitata) *in Cameroon. The monkey-bread tree, as it is also known, produces sausage-shaped fruit 6 to 10 inches long and 4 inches wide that are eaten by wild animals and natives. The fibrous bark of the baobab is used to make fish nets and clothing.* (Klaus Paysan)

54 *overleaf. Symbol of the East African savannahs, the umbrella-shaped camel thorn* (Acacia giraffe) *is well suited for life in an arid environment. Its small leaves conserve precious water, and its roots may spread to a depth of 80 feet to tap groundwater supplies. Giraffes are fond of the camel thorn's foliage and seed pods, but both contain hydrocyanic acid that under certain conditions proves fatal to wildlife and domestic livestock. The name "camel thorn" refers to the giraffe's scientific name,* Giraffa camelopardalis. (R. I. M. Campbell/Bruce Coleman, Ltd.)

57 *above. Standing on its hind legs, a gerenuk* (Litocrarius walleri) *browses the leaves of an acacia. This dainty African antelope with the long thin neck is so well balanced that it can stand without supporting its front legs against a tree trunk or branches.*
(Hans D. Dossenbach)

56. *A Masai giraffe* (Giraffa camelopardalis tippelskirchi) *on the Tanzanian plain. The giraffe fears few other animals. Even lions are vulnerable to skull-crushing blows from its powerful front legs. But the blunt horns, not feet, are used in skirmishes between male giraffes for supremacy in a herd; serious injuries are rare.* (Stewart Cassidy)

57 *above. A female night ape* (Galago senegalensis mohali) *peers from its home in a hollow Terminalia tree. Galagos, or bush-babies, are small lemurs that live in natural cavities or old wood-pecker holes throughout Africa's savannah woodlands. But the felling of dead and dying trees for firewood threatens these and other hole-nesting creatures. Bushbabies are omnivorous, but feed extensively on insects.*
(D. C. H. Plowes)

58 *above. A weaver constructs a nest in Zimbabwe. There are some 150 species of sparrow-size songbirds in the Ploceidae family, most of them found in Africa south of the Sahara. As many as 300 strands of grass will be skillfully worked into a weaver's nest; a "guard rail" around the breeding chamber keeps the eggs from tumbling out the entrance hole at the bottom.* (Thomas Nebbia)

58 *right. A baya weaver (Ploceus philippinus) leaves its nest via a long entrance tube that leads to a breeding chamber. Ranging from Pakistan and India to Thailand and Sumatra, the baya weaver nests in large colonies. Males construct the tightly woven nests, which are excellent protection against predation by snakes or monkeys.* (Stanley Breeden)

59. *Some 3 dozen weaver nests hang from a thorn tree (Acacia tortilis) in Kenya's Nairobi National Park. Rather than individual nests, the sociable weavers of South Africa construct huge haystack "apartment houses" in the branches of isolated veldt trees; more than 100 pairs of weavers will have their nest chambers under one roof.* (Edward S. Ross)

60 *overleaf. African elephants (Loxodonta africana) in Amboseli National Park, Kenya. The food needs of an elephant weighing several tons are tremendous. It spends 16 of every 24 hours grazing and browsing, consuming one-sixth of a ton of vegetation every day.* (Lynn McLaren/N.A.S./Photo Researchers, Inc.)

62 *second overleaf. Doum palms (Hyphaene theobaica) at Meru National Park, Kenya, have branched trunks—a rare shape among palm trees. Growing to a height of 30 feet, the doum palm was cultivated by the earliest civilizations in Egypt and the Sudan. Ancient Egyptians con-sidered the tree sacred; and it provides nourishing fruit, with ivorylike seeds that are carved into such items as buttons. Though doum palms grow best near good groundwater supplies, they can survive desert heat.* (Sven-Olof Lindblad/N.A.S./Photo Researchers, Inc.)

65 *above. Formidable spines arm the trunk of a taborichi* (Chorisia ventricosa). *This genus of only 5 trees, all found in the dry, tropical woodlands of Brazil and Argentina, belongs to the bombax family which includes the kapok and balsa trees.* (Tony Morrison)

64. *A grove of* campo cerrado *trees in the Mato Grosso of Brazil. This vast plateau of sandstone overlain with clay is typified by savannahs that are sprinkled with clumps of trees. On the Mato Grosso, extremely dry seasons alternate with wet seasons when rainfall totals more than 70 inches.* (Francois Gohier)

65 *above. Similarly protected by innumerable spines is the floss-silk tree* (Chorisia speciosa), *whose seed pods produce a floss used for the same purposes as the kapok from the silk-cotton tree.* (Walter H. Hodge)

66 *overleaf. Burchell's zebras* (Equus quagga burchelli) *congregate at a Kenya waterhole. The zebra's stark pattern is highly visible during the day, accounting for the nervousness of this wild horse of the savannahs; but it becomes almost invisible at dusk when lions are on the prowl.* (Susan McCartney/N.A.S./Photo Researchers, Inc.

68. *Spring foliage is reflected in a cypress pond near Charleston, South Carolina. Bald cypress* (Taxodium distichum) *may thrive in riverbottom forests or in broad, blackwater swamps where the downhill flow of coffee-colored (but potable and harmless) water is barely perceptible.*
(Sonja Bullaty)

Galleries of Life:
The Riverside Trees

"It is still, hot, oppressive scenery, except when
we come to rivers." So wrote the English missionary
David Livingstone as he journeyed across Africa
in 1855. Where so much of the world is treeless,
where plains stretch for miles and deserts disappear
in mirages, the rivers and their forests, air-conditioned
by nature, provide welcome relief to man and beast.
Often the only trees for miles around grow in snaking
lines that coincide with the banks of streams. As we
canoe down the river it seems as though we float
through an immense art gallery—trunks of trees
rise up like marble columns, and frescoes of leaves
and limbs dance in the sunlight.

In Africa, these streambank woods, densely packed
with large trees, resemble (or are) tropical rain
forests. In the Ivory Coast the species characteristic
of riverbanks include *Cynometra megalophylla* and
Hymenostegia emarginata. The 2,375,000-acre
Upemba National Park, Zaïre, supports several
systems of river forests: at low elevations the
mahogany (*Khaya*) and fig trees grow, while a bit
higher, gallery forests of raffia palms (*Raphia*) and
bamboo (*Bambusa*) thrive.

Some distance away from the river these dense woods
may end abruptly. Few natural forest boundaries
are so pronounced; the contrast could hardly be
greater. A thick tangle of tropical woods suddenly
gives way to grassland or savanna or desert.
The secret lies in the availability of water to
the roots.

One of the most lively and interesting riverine
forests is that along the Rapti and Narayani rivers in

the Royal Chitwan National Park, Nepal. Dominating thick lowland woods are khair (*Acacia catechu*), a fairly large thorn tree, and sissoo (*Dalbergia sissoo*), a tree, sometimes 60 feet tall, bearing vivid green leaves. These two trees colonize wet places and stabilize the sand and gravel. The simal tree (*Bombax malabaricum*) then becomes established and forms a strip of woods behind the khair-sissoo association. Rhesus monkeys spend their nights in the trees of the riverine forest, in daylight descending to the ground to hunt for insects and vegetable matter. Langurs, arboreal monkeys that travel in troops of twenty or so, are prime prey for leopards.

On our travels by elephant through these river forests we often met the great one-horned rhinoceros, snorting and plunging into the water for a swim, or grazing in small meadows beneath the trees. Deer slip secretively through the shadows or stand camouflaged in the shrubbery. All of the deer—sambar, barking, hog, and chital— are at home in the riverbank woodlands. So are peafowl, red jungle fowl, and a host of other birds.

During the day many of these animals may move from the lowlands into the surrounding hills, which are covered with forests of sal (*Shorea robusta*). This huge, straight-trunked deciduous tree may grow to a height of 150 feet, but more commonly reaches about 80 feet. It looms above the dense grass (*Themeda caudata*) which grows 20 feet high on the forest floor. Sal trees bear sprays of white flowers and put out new leaves in March, but though deciduous, they are never quite leafless. Notable for growing in pure stands across much of Asia, they may sometimes be found with a few other trees, such as *Terminalia*.

In northern Australia, tropical rain forests would be far more widespread were it not for the extreme seasonal pattern of precipitation. As it is, gallery forests along permanent watercourses are the only places where dense forest associations exist. Elsewhere, gallery stands of coachwood (*Ceratopetalum apetalum*) may be found in sheltered, nutrient-enriched valleys and gorges such as those in Morton and Blue Mountains National Parks.

In drier lands the tree most apt to flourish is river red gum (*Eucalyptus camaldulensis*), said to be the most widespread, best known, and probably best loved of all Australian eucalypts. It occurs in every state except Tasmania, a fascinating tree, large, gnarled, and wide-spreading; but a picnic under it can be hazardous. It has a tendency to drop its limbs unexpectedly, particularly in hot weather.

Some of the paperbarks (*Melaleuca*) thrive in the swampy and brackish soils of Australian wetlands. Here and there they grow in nearly pure stands on riverbanks, estuaries, and even in lagoons where their roots are immersed in water. Narrowleaf paperbarks (*M. linariifolia*) bloom with such a profusion of white flowers that they seem to be blanketed with snow. Cajuput trees (*M. leucadendra*) do well in waterlogged brackish soils. Kangaroo tea trees (*M. halmaturorum*) exist on the edges of salt lagoons. White paperbarks (*M. cuticularis*), with their gleaming white trunks, stand out sharply in swamplands and wet soils. Even an occasional acacia grows along the river bottoms, especially the river cooba or eumong (*Acacia stenophylla*).

The same laws of nature apply to North American streams, but there are no native eucalypts or melaleucas. Instead, a sandy, gravelly streambed in, say, central Arizona grows thickly with sycamore (*Platanus wrightii*) and cottonwood (*Populus fremontii*). The riverbed sands have a favorable water-retaining capacity and the creeks constitute a fairly dependable supply of moisture year-round, even though water may flow only underground during drier seasons. The riverine woods are dense with wild grape tangles (*Vitis*), hackberry (*Celtis reticulata*), walnut (*Juglans major*), and alder (*Alnus oblongifolia*).

A swamp is very often part of a river system and the water, however dark and serene, may have a vigorous current. Wetlands are flowing systems—moisture, nutrients, and debris flow through them (as well as pollutants, alas). One of North America's largest swamps, the Okefenokee, in the state of Georgia, is now a national wildlife refuge. The swamp measures 38 miles across. Its waters, brown with organic matter, are the source of the Suwannee River. Canoeing through intricate waterways, we pass beneath huge branches of bald cypress (*Taxodium distichum*) with fluted trunks, woody "knees" that protrude from the shallow root system, and a gallery of Spanish moss (*Tillandsia*)—a member of the pineapple family—hanging in curtains from the limbs. Thousands of alligators live here, and in the pines at the fringe of the swamp the red-cockaded woodpecker may be found. Bottomland forest along the lower White River, in southeastern Arkansas, is widely regarded as among the finest in the huge Mississippi River basin. The region is subject to frequent and prolonged flooding, occasionally to a depth of 25 feet, which makes it unsuitable for cultivation or settlement. A labyrinth of channels connects with major rivers; there are 169 lakes in the White River National Wildlife Refuge. In this quiet milieu massive bald cypress trees rise out of the brown waters. Typical along the bayous are water tupelo (*Nyssa aquatica*), with its buttressed trunks; water locust (*Gleditsia aquatica*), a tall spiny-twigged legume; the planer tree (*Planera aquatica*), an inconspicuous member of the elm family; and the water hickory or bitter pecan (*Carya aquatica*). Many other trees share these riverine woodlands, and well they should. The silt of centuries has rendered the soils exceptionally rich, which means that the productivity can be tremendous. One old oak once produced more than 28,000 acorns in a single year.

Finally, there are the hammocks, islands of trees in the Everglades of southern Florida. This broad grassland is in reality a wide marshy river, 6 inches deep, and 50 miles from one side to the other, flowing 100 miles from Lake Okeechobee to Florida Bay. The shallow waters normally sift through saw grass and willow except where outcrops of limestone rise just a few inches above the water. There dense forests spring up, their trees more characteristic of the West Indies than of Florida. Most conspicuous are gumbo-limbo (*Bursera simaruba*), with multiple twisted arms and copper-colored bark, and royal palm (*Roystonea elata*), a towering straight-trunked tree that lives up to its name. There are also bustic (*Dipholis salicifolia*), live oak (*Quercus virginiana*), mastic (*Sideroxylon foetidissimum*) and mahogany (*Swietenia mahagoni*), as well as a host of smaller trees beneath them, all strung with orchids and air plants. The Spanish name for these hammocks, *hamaca*, can in fact be taken as descriptive of many riverside forests around the world. It means "garden place."

73. *Moss-draped bald cypress rim a Texas bayou. Because of great demand for its durable wood, few virgin stands of bald cypress survived the loggers' axes. But two of the world's finest cypress swamps are preserved in National Audubon Society sanctuaries in South Carolina and Florida. Cypress wood was used to make barrels and caskets, for shingles, as railroad ties, and bridge beams. Cypress heartwood is virtually indestructible, and small fortunes have been made salvaging sunken logs left from oldtime timbering operations.* (David Muench)

76 *overleaf. Spongy, knobby knees that grow upward from submerged cypress roots remain an enigma to botanists. One theory is that the knees, some of them several feet high, help aerate the waterlogged roots. Another claim is that the knees help stabilize the cypress in its mucky anchorage. No proof exists for either explanation.* (John Shaw)

74 *and* **75.** *Bald cypress is a deciduous relative of the giant, evergreen redwoods and sequoias of the Pacific Coast forests, and its featherlike foliage turns yellow or a rich brown before dropping in autumn. Though such specimens are rare today, a thousand-year-old cypress will stand 150 feet tall with a tapered trunk 12 feet in diameter. Swamp cypress in particular have massive supporting buttresses that are used as resting places by turtles, snakes, and even deer.* (74 James P. Valentine; 75 John Shaw)

78 and **79.** *A bald cypress without its curtains of Spanish moss* (Tillandsia usneoides) *would be like a Christmas tree without garlands. Not a moss at all, but an epiphyte and a member of the pineapple family,* Tillandsia *is a rootless plant that draws its sustenance from the air and rain. It spreads by producing seeds from tiny but aromatic flowers, and by shedding bits of moss in heavy winds. A piece of Spanish moss landing on another branch will grow an inch every month.*
(78 Wendell D. Metzen; 79 both John Eastcott/Yva Momatiuk)

80 *overleaf. Fog lifting from Louisiana's Atchafalaya Swamp reveals an eerie scene—rotting buttresses of bald cypress cut long ago for lumber, and a few surviving trees truncated by hurricane winds. In coastal swamps, ancient cypress with picture-perfect shapes are rare indeed; most old trees have been decapitated in raging storms.*
(John Eastcott/Yva Momatiuk)

82. *In Georgia's famed Okefenokee Swamp, the yellow flowers of floating bladderwort* (Utricularia inflata) *rise above the water, the stems supported by wheels of inflated leaf stalks. The plant receives nourishment from the bodies of small aquatic animals that are trapped by tiny bladders on its submerged leaves.*
(Wendell D. Metzen)

83. *A strangler fig* (Ficus aurea) *embraces a mahogany tree* (Swietenia mahogani) *on a hammock in Everglades National Park. The sticky seed of a strangler fig will become lodged in a crotch on a host tree and send down aerial roots that eventually reach the ground. The roots enlarge and become the fig's own trunk when the host tree perishes.*
(Sonja Bullaty)

84. *A barking tree frog (Hyla gratiosa) is poised on the trunk of a cabbage palmetto (Sabal palmetto) in Florida's Big Cypress Swamp. Official state tree of Florida, the cabbage palmetto is native to seacoast woodlands from North Carolina to Florida. It reaches a height of 75 feet, its bark usually hidden beneath dead leaf bases.* (Patricia Caulfield)

85. *Long-lasting dead leaf bases hide the bark of a cabbage palmetto (Sabal palmetto) in the Florida Everglades. Growing to a height of 75 feet in sun or shade, this is one of 20 species of palmetto palms. All are found in the New World, on Caribbean islands or adjacent mainland coasts.* (Sonja Bullaty)

86 *overleaf. Water tupelos* (Nyssa aquatica) *line a bayou off the lower Mississippi River, while ranks of loblolly pines* (Pinus taeda) *face the main channel, where a broad beach has been scoured by spring floods. Often called sour gum, the water tupelo is found on rich bottomlands along the coastal plain from Virginia to Texas, and north along the Mississippi Valley to southern Illinois. It occurs in pure stands or mixed with bald cypress and oaks. The dark purple fruits, prized by turkeys and many song-birds, are distributed by the streams into which they fall. A common tree of the southeastern United States, loblolly pine is widely used for pulp and building construction.* (Harald Sund)

88. *Brilliant sunlight reveals the structure of a cabbage palmetto leaf* (Sabal palmetto) *on Bull's Island, Georgia. Nearly circular, 3 to 6 feet long, the fan-shaped leaf is divided into many narrow, long-pointed segments that radiate from a long stalk. Cabbage palmettos are common along the coast from the Florida Keys to North Carolina; this slow-growing species is easy to cultivate as a lawn tree.* (Sonja Bullaty)

89. *The leaf of a sweetgum* (Liquidambar styraciflua) *is silhouetted against a palmetto fan. Sweetgum is a common tree of bottomlands and floodplains in the southeastern United States, and a sweet-smelling resin obtained*

from its bark once was used in soaps, cosmetics, and adhesives. (John Shaw)

90 *overleaf. Texas palmettos* (Sabal texana) *rise over the Rio Grande Valley near the Mexican border. Restricted to extreme south Texas and northeastern Mexico, this species of palm grows to a height of 50 feet on a stout, column-shaped trunk. Its leaves are used for thatch and baskets.* (David Muench)

92. *The skeleton of an ancient live oak* (Quercus virginiana), *remnant of a forest long ago overtaken by the sea, salutes dawn on the Georgia coastal island of Ossabaw. The weathered limbs may stand for decades; the wood of live oak is so strong and worm-resistant that it was prized by early shipbuilders. It is the heaviest native hardwood in North America, weighing 55 pounds per cubic foot when dry.* (James P. Valentine)

Coasts and Islands: The Fantasy Trees

Rarely is nature more specialized than on islands. If islands are geologically or topographically complex, the number of endemic species may be extraordinary. For example, in the Canary Islands, off the west coast of Africa, there are cliffs and volcanic crags where no botanist has been, and where, leading Spanish botanists say, new species of plants undoubtedly exist. The names of many trees indicate their specialization on islands: *Pinus canariensis*, *Palma canariensis*, and *Euphorbia canariensis*, named for the Canary Islands, *Laurus azorica*, named for the Azores, and so on.

Let us visit some relatively tiny islands in the South Pacific Ocean. They look like something out of *Tales of the South Pacific*—idyllic, uninhabited, tropical paradises where time seems to stop. Typical is Wilson Island, on the Great Barrier Reef in the western Pacific. It is low and flat, scarcely 8 feet above sea level and 2 miles in circumference. Trees cover it thickly, their presence the result of more than one method of long-distance seed dispersal.

All looks peaceful. But paradise it is not. At midday the sun can be excruciatingly hot. As in deserts, drought is normal; there is little or no fresh water on or under the island. Occasional cyclones wreck the forest. Too much salt spray can sear tree leaves at any time.

As we climb up the white coral beach we first encounter a grove of casuarina trees (*Casuarina equisetifolia*), one of many so-called "she-oaks" native to Australia. Their limbs are limp, their slender branchlets sway with the breeze and offer little

resistance to the wind. Yet they constitute a
kind of windbreak that protects the
interior woods.

Next we come to pandanus, or screw pine (*Pandanus*),
trees more sturdy and able to stand their ground
because of proplike roots that spread out like the
legs of a tripod. Another tough but low-spreading
tree that exists along the outer fringe is *Messer-
schmidtia argentea*. Behind these trees lies the
interior. We enter a grove of *Pisonia grandis*,
a sprawling, huge-limbed tree whose green and
yellow leaves filter the sunlight and create a golden
environment. Even the strong, solid trunk and
branches, which twist and curve almost down to the
ground, are cream-colored. The limbs take root when
they touch the ground; hence a tree blown down
generates several new trees.

Ordinarily, this is a quiet environment, but in
September and October on nearby Heron Island the
Pisonia woods resound with a day-and-night racket of
croaks and rattles almost unbearable to human ears.
This is when the white-capped noddy terns nest
in the trees and breed by the thousands. While they
are present, their droppings fertilize the sand,
which helps account for the robust growth of *Pisonia*
trees; in effect, they transfer nutrients from the ocean,
where they feed, to the forest, where they nest.
They also rub against the sticky seeds of *Pisonia*,
which cling to their feathers and are thereby
dispersed to other islands. (Sometimes the birds
perish when they get so covered with seeds that they
cannot fly.) Thus the tern and *Pisonia* constitute a
fine example of ecological collaboration on these
sandy terrestrial outposts in a huge ocean. They also
suggest one means by which trees spread among
oceanic islands many miles apart.

In French Polynesia, 4,000 miles east, the outposts
of land are relatively larger and are, for the most
part, of volcanic rather than coralline origin. The
mountain soils are not very fertile and so support
mostly ferns. Here and there are wild bananas in
ravines, and in upland thickets is the small puarata
tree (*Metrosideros collina*), its bright scarlet flowers
identical to the ohia-lehua of Hawaii. The coasts and
valleys possess a more exuberant vegetation—most
of it Indo-Malaysian in origin.

One of the most conspicuous trees is the breadfruit
(*Artocarpus altilis*), recognized by its large, glossy,

sharp-pointed leaves and abundant green fruit. Its origin, like that of the banana, is uncertain but seems to lie in Southeast Asia or Melanesia. So nourishing and plentiful was the fruit—Captain Cook described its many advantages—that the British dispatched Captain William Bligh on the *Bounty* to take breadfruit from the Society Islands to the Antilles. He dropped anchor in Matavai Bay in 1788 and took to sea six months later with 1,015 breadfruit trees aboard. That is when the well-known mutiny occurred. Four years later Bligh returned, and this time he loaded 2,500 trees on two ships and took them to the West Indies.

The artificial distribution of trees by man has gone on steadily in the past three centuries. The islands of French Polynesia, for example, are virtually microcosms of world flora, especially of the more colorful and fantastic species.

One of the most fantastic is the traveler's tree (*Ravenala madagascariensis*), originally from the Malay peninsula. A member of the banana family, this tree has a palmlike trunk and fronds that spread out like a giant fan 30 feet above the ground. The remarkable spreading roots of Tahitian chestnut (*Inocarpus edulis*), from the East Indies, have vertical ridges that give the appearance of an intricate maze. Poinsettia (*Euphorbia pulcherrima*), native to Mexico and Central America, is often thought of only as a potted Christmas plant, but here it grows to tree height. The flowers are inconspicuous but the scarlet bracts give the plant a flamelike hue. Giant bamboo (*Dendrocalamus giganteus*), from Southeast Asia, is a huge grass that reaches tree proportions and can grow 20 inches in a day. Then there are the mango (*Mangifera indica*) and banyan tree (*Ficus benghalensis*) from India and several frangipanis (*Plumeria*) from tropical America. The list goes on and on.

The most prominent tree on Tahitian coasts—and on many other coasts, for that matter—is the coconut palm (*Cocos nucifera*). Its seeds are so capable of floating and growing throughout the world that no one knows where it originated. Without it, the squirrels and monkeys and other wildlife of the world would have a difficult existence—they use it for food and shelter. Man has developed more than a thousand uses for it (food, fuel, drink, shelter, tools, torches, oil, paints, medicine, fishing nets). A coconut palm may produce up to 450 fruits a year and live for a hundred years. When one considers optimum growth of, say, 50 coconut palms on a single acre, that is a remarkable production of 22,500 coconuts per acre per year. In French Polynesia the coconut palm extends from coasts into estuaries and rivers and part way up the slopes of mountains. Vast numbers of them have 18-inch collars of metal wrapped around their trunks perhaps 15 feet above the ground. Puzzled, we asked the Tahitians why, and the answer was simple. "Rats." Were it not for the collar, these introduced mammals would climb to the delicate growing tip of the palm and eat it out.

Coconuts may float for thousands of miles in the sea, then wash ashore, take root, and grow. It is a success story matched only by another saltwater coastal tree distributed in both tropic and temperate regions: the mangrove (*Rhizophora, Bruguiera, Avicennia, Laguncularia*). For all or most of their lives mangroves are rooted in salt water or in a salty substratum. Multiple roots are sent down, like huge fingers clutching the sand; hence the tree is fixed in place and remains when all else blows away in hurricanes or cyclones.

The marvels of trees adapted to the rigors of coastal life can be observed far beyond the tropics or subtropics. Journeys north along the Atlantic shore reveal changing conditions that trees are nevertheless prepared for. There is yaupon (*Ilex vomitoria*) in North Carolina, pine (*Pinus*) and Atlantic white cedar (*Chamaecyparis thyoides*) on Cape Cod in Massachusetts, spruce (*Picea*) on the granite shores of Maine. And on the Pacific Coast— trees of desert, fog, and rain forest.

Why do they grow there? Pruned by high winds, shriveled by drought, burned by salt spray, inundated by waves, uprooted in shifting sands: how *can* they grow there? As well ask: why survive? They are there because few or no other trees grow in coastal environments, because the continuous adaptations of their ancestors for thousands of years made them tough enough and flexible enough to come through all the trials—alive if not well—and then reproduce. Man is still trying to make a product as durable.

97. *Slowly, inexorably, a sand dune slides toward a fog-shrouded coastal forest on Georgia's Cumberland Island. Its first victim will be a gnarled southern redcedar* (Juniperus silicicola) *whose branches bridge a seasonal rain pond. Redcedars bear male and female flowers on separate trees. Large crops of sweet, blue berry-like cones are produced once every three years and are a food bonanza for wild turkeys, quail, and songbirds.* (James P. Valentine)

98 *overleaf. On the Indian Ocean atoll of Aldabra, famed for its population of giant tortoises, a black mangrove* (Avicennia sp.) *spreads its tentaclelike root system. Pencil-thin spikes that jut above the mud, botanists believe, help the mangrove roots to breathe. The mangroves that fringe tropical shores around the world not only secure the land against the incessant assault of the sea; they are absolutely vital, in countless ways, to the lives of a myriad of creatures—from nesting eagles to tiny crustaceans.* (Robert Hernandez/N.A.S./Photo Researchers, Inc.)

100. *Stiltlike roots of a red mangrove* (Rhizophora mangle) *are anchored in the mud of a tidal bay on the Guatemala coast. Mangrove bark has been utilized for tanning leather and for dyes and medicines. Its strong wood is used for fenceposts, fuel, even cabinet-making. Fallen mangrove leaves, meanwhile, form a nutrient-rich detritus that feeds a wide variety of marine life.* (Steven C. Wilson/Entheos)

102 *overleaf. Nesting wood storks congregate in the tops of mangroves along the Lane River in Everglades National Park. Once widespread across the southern United States, the wood stork has been reduced in this century from 100,000 breeding pairs to perhaps 3,000 pairs today. Lumbering of cypress forest and drainage of Florida wetlands are prime causes of this disastrous decline. Three and one-half feet tall, wood storks walk about freshwater ponds on their long legs, eating fish, frogs, snakes, young alligators, and aquatic insects.* (Caulion Singletary)

101. *Hidden deep in a tangle of mangroves on Bottle Key, in Everglades National Park, is the nest of a roseate spoonbill* (Ajaia ajaja). *The mangrove-clad islands of Florida Bay are host to spectacular colonies of spoonbills, herons, egrets, pelicans, and frigatebirds—plus the nests of bald eagles and ospreys. Rare crocodiles dig their nests on the keys' sandy shores.* (Caulion Singletary)

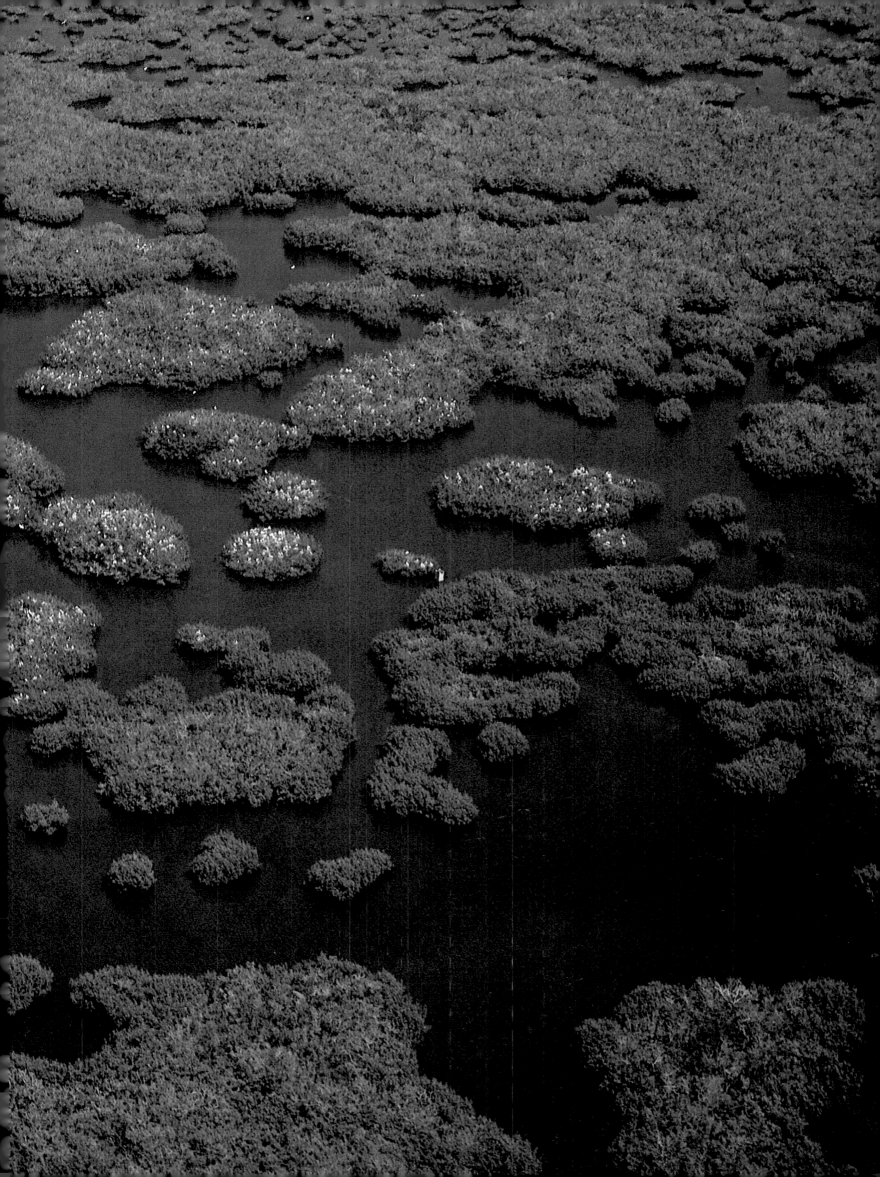

104. *Endemic to the volcanic islands off the northwest coast of Africa, Canary Island pines* (Pinus canariensis) *thrive on such dry, open slopes as this caldera on La Palma. Canary Island pines are noted for drooping needles up to a foot in length and giant cones 8 to 9 inches long.* (Stephanie Dinkins/N.A.S./Photo Researchers, Inc.)

105. *Towering ohia lehua trees* (Metrosideros polymorpha) *dominate rain-drenched Alakai Swamp on the Hawaiian island of Kauai. A depression on the side of an ancient volcano, Mount Waialeale, Alakai Swamp may receive 50 feet of rain a year. In such places, ohia lehua trees reach*

a height of 100 feet. But on rocky, dry mountain slopes, a fully mature ohia lehua may be no more than a shrub a foot tall. (Harald Sund)

106 *overleaf. Live oaks* (Quercus virginiana) *populate a motte, or hillock, that rises a few feet above a brackish marsh at Aransas National Wildlife Refuge on the Texas coast. Aransas is world-famous as the wintering place for the largest flock of whooping cranes, now numbering more than 70 birds. But the refuge is a cornucopia of wildlife, including such other rare species as the red wolf and Attwater's prairie chicken.* (David Muench)

108. *One of the largest plants in the Agavaceae, a family that includes only a handful of trees, is the cabbage tree (Cordyline australis) of New Zealand cloud forests. The popular name of this 40-foot-high tree reflects the edible nature of its fleshy roots. The leathery, palmlike leaves were utilized by Maoris for making paper and rope. Wild pigeons relish the cabbage tree's milky white berries.* (Kjell B. Sandved)

Among the Giants: Trees of Temperate Rain Forests

Now meet the stinging tree. And the carrabin, coachwood, redwood, red cedar, and alerce. They live awash in the cool mists of temperate climes. Their environment is one of rain that pours for days on end and keeps them soaked. Or fog that sifts through the woods and drenches them so thoroughly that their leaves and branches seem perpetually strung with droplets. Rot doesn't bother them. Fire has little effect. Freezing is seldom a problem. Winds rarely rage. The soils are usually rich. It would appear logical that in such a paradise, trees could go on living forever. And they do—if a thousand years seems like forever. But they have problems, not the least of which is lack of water. That is only one anomaly of temperate rain forests.

On the Wonga Walk into Dorrigo National Park, one abruptly realizes that Australia is not all desert. Far from it. Here in the mountains of New South Wales remain a few patches of rain forest which, though mere remnants when compared to what once existed in the region, seem anything but small to the visitor. It is virtually impossible to see to the tops of these trees unless one finds some opening where he can look out, say, to the other side of this huge, deep, densely wooded canyon. Standing beside the red cedar (*Toona australis*), some specimens of which are known to reach a height of nearly 230 feet with trunk diameters of 10 feet, we can appreciate how much minerals, moisture, and undisturbed quiet went into the making of such a giant. The giant coachwood (*Ceratopetalum apetalum*) grew in nearly pure stands in the original Australian rain forests.

All is not gloom, for color is strong, especially when the spectacular Dorrigo waratah (*Oreocallis pinnata*) blooms. Its bright red flowers measure nearly 5 inches across. Australian rain forests are also endowed with orchids; the lovely orange blossom orchid (*Sarcochilus falcatus*) bears white flowers with red and yellow centers. Nearly everywhere the woods are luxuriant with mosses, lichens, and fungi; few plants, however, are as prominent as the elkhorn fern (*Platycerium grande*). It and other ferns become attached to the huge trunks of trees and send out such a mass of fronds that the tree seems to be wearing a skirt. Sometimes even the trunks of the trees are nearly invisible because of all the clinging vines and leaves of other plants.

As we descend into the ravine, we pass huge tree trunks such as that of the yellow carrabin (*Sloanea australis*), which develops enormous plank buttresses at the base of the trunk. The tree appears to send out curved walls of wood to support its weight, an aboveground development of the root system. But no one knows the function of these buttresses. That is a common problem in contemporary rain forest knowledge: there has been too little functional analysis. We often know what happens but not why. One reason for our lack of knowledge is the difficulty of carrying on field work. Australian rain forests are not particularly hospitable to people. Vines and lianas impede progress. Leaves and flowers are usually high above ground. A human observer must peel off ticks and leeches. He may have an acutely painful encounter with the stinging tree (*Dendrocnide excelsa*), another giant—up to 160 feet tall. The large round leaves of this tree bear small hairs that, when touched, penetrate the skin and inject an irritating acid. Then there are centipedes, spiders, and scorpions.

Despite the giant and diversified growth, temperate rain forests around the world can sometimes be subject to a dearth of water. Tropical rain forests seldom have this problem; their continuity of function is based on a stable and continuous year-round fall of rain. But temperate rain forest functions may be subject to interruption. If climatic cycles produce a season when little or no rain falls and the forest dries out, each species present, plant and animal, must be fit to endure. Extreme winds can accompany cyclones and open the forest, although, by and large, rain forests spring up in sheltered places where weather conditions are less hazardous.

One such place, in the shadow of the Andes, is Los Alerces National Park, Argentina. Here grows a forest of alerces (*Fitzroya cupressoides*), a giant, whose tall straight trunk is shrouded in mists for much of the year. Some of the trees are evidently over a thousand years old. Though the tree is presently common enough in Chile, Argentine scientists think these pockets on the eastern side of the Andes are on their way to extinction. The reason, they say, is that the habitat is slowly but inexorably shrinking—and has been for perhaps millennia. It is a colorful forest, especially with its bright green bamboos about the bases of the trees and the attractive arrayán tree (*Myrceugenella apiculata*) with its orange bark. All around these secluded groves spreads the immense southern beech forest, composed mostly of coihue (*Nothofagus dombeyi*). This is a highly successful woods but drier then the rain forest and extremely susceptible to fire.

Although temperate rain forests have reached a greater degree of complexity in the Southern Hemisphere, a few magnificent rain forests have developed in the Northern Hemisphere, principally on the Pacific Coast of North America. Without doubt, the masterpiece of all rain forest trees—at least in terms of height—is the California coast redwood (*Sequoia sempervirens*), which may grow up to 367 feet tall, 14 feet in diameter, and reach 2,000 years of age. Seldom farther than 30 miles inland, groves of redwood occur in protected vales from central California to southern Oregon.

Four hundred miles farther north, in western Washington, lie the rain forests of the Olympic Peninsula. A heavy influx of moisture, in places exceeding 140 inches each year, comes from the Pacific Ocean. The result is water, water everywhere—and some of the densest vegetation in North America. Four conifers dominate. The Sitka spruce (*Picea sitchensis*), a common coastal tree between Washington and Alaska, may reach 200 feet in height. The slightly smaller western hemlock (*Tsuga heterophylla*) may be identified by a nodding topmost branch. It is more common throughout the montane Pacific region. The Douglas fir (*Pseudotsuga menziesii*) is an immense tree—up to 250 feet tall—

that is highly valued commercially. It is common from Mexico almost to Alaska. Also commercially valuable, the western red cedar (*Thuja plicata*) bears closest resemblance to the alerces of Argentine fog forests; they are both in the cypress family.

But Olympic rain forests are by no means limited to these giant conifers. They are in fact so filled with alder (*Alnus rubra*), vine maple (*Acer circinatum*), and other deciduous trees that a layer of leaves within 20 feet or so of the forest floor alters the gray light into yellow-green. It is one of the most intense and cheerful greens of any rain forest environment. Moreover, sphagnum moss grows on practically everything—dead or alive—in the forest. The environment is rich enough to support more than a hundred species of mosses and liverworts and nearly seventy species of lichens. Curtains of moss hang from the branches of trees, and carpets of it cling to trunks and logs.

Northward into Canada, rain forests hug the Pacific coast or develop in mountain ravines sheltered from coastal winds. Were it not for the mild influence of oceanic waters, the gentle luxuriant forests would extend no farther north than perhaps California. As it is, they press on through British Columbia and into the southeastern Alaska panhandle. We can observe their evolution in Glacier Bay, where glaciers have retreated 65 miles inland within the last two centuries. After mats of avens (*Dryas drummondii*) give way to thickets of alder (*Alnus*) and cottonwood (*Populus*), the Sitka spruce springs forth and in due course becomes the dominant tree species.

There is no end to the fascination of rain forests with their rich and delicate abundance of flora. The trees are so huge and so old that they seem to have been there forever. We would like to think that they will always be there. But the forests have been widely wiped out in the past, and because we know that human settlement can develop rapidly, we cannot be certain that they will endure. As the Greek philosopher Arcesilaus said 2,000 years ago: "Nothing is certain, not even that."

113. *Three hundred inches of rain falls annually on the forests of Mount Egmont, an 8,260-foot dormant volcano on New Zealand's North Island. Common names for many of the trees of this temperate rain forest come from the Maori language: rimu, totara, rata, kowhai. Totaras* (Podocarpus totara) *are massive evergreen conifers whose trunks were hollowed out by Maoris to make 70-foot-long war canoes. Its durable wood is used for wharf pilings, for it is highly resistent to marine teredo worms.* (Walter H. Hodge)

114. *Rimu or red-pine* (Pinus resinosa) *is an important timber tree in New Zealand forests, attaining a height of 100 feet with a trunk diameter of 5 feet. The leaves of this conifer are described as "little more than small prickles pointing along the slender drooping stems." This rimu is embraced, perhaps fatally, by a strangling rata* (Metrosideros robusta), *which begins life as a epiphyte germinated from a wind-borne seed caught in the high branches of its host. The roots that the rata sends toward the earth thicken and engulf the tree like a corset.* (Walter H. Hodge)

115. *A famous tree on New Zealand's North Island is this kauri pine* (Agathis australis).

Known as "Tanemahuta," a Maori word meaning "God-of-the-Forest," it is 169 feet high, 44 feet in diameter, and 1,200 years old. Kauri pine and its relatives are important timber trees in New Zealand, Australia, and the East Indies; and their resin is used in making paint, varnish, and linoleum. (Walter H. Hodge)

116 *overleaf. Vine maple* (Acer circinatum) *is a familiar understory shrub or tree in the Pacific Coast rain forests from British Columbia to California. Rarely taller than 50 feet, often twisted or sprawling over the ground, it is one of the few deciduous trees in this largely evergreen world.* (Steven C. Wilson/Entheos)

118. *Botanists named vine maple* Acer circinatum *because of the rounded shape of its bright green leaves. Its company in the rain-soaked, west-facing forests of the Pacific Northwest—redwoods, Sitka spruce, Douglas-fir, western redcedar—are among the most important timber trees on Earth. But vine maple has little practical use except as firewood for coastal residents.* (Harald Sund)

119 *left. New yellow-green needles are crowded on a branchlet of Douglas-fir* (Pseudotsuga menziesii), *one of the most important timber trees in the Pacific rain forest. The 5 species of Douglas-firs— two in North America, three in Asia—are not true firs but occupy a separate genus. The common name honors the Scottish botanist David Douglas, who explored North America from 1823 to 1834 and sent back plants and seeds of more than 200 species then unknown to European scientists. Douglas was one of the first travelers in the wilds of Oregon and California.* (Steven C. Wilson/ Entheos)

119 *right. Eight-inch-long leaves of false Solomon's seal* (Smilacina racemosa), *in the Oregon rain forest, alternate along a reclining stem. A dense cluster of tiny white flowers at the tip of the stem produces red berries in autumn. A member of the lily family, false Solomon's seal is found in moist woodlands across cool, temperate North America.* (Gary Braasch)

120 *overleaf. Shiny, heart-shaped leaves crowded about the base of a Douglas-fir* (Pseudotsuga menziesii) *on Vancouver Island, British Columbia, belong to wild lily-of-the-valley* (Maianthemum kamtschaticum), *a plant commonly found in moist conifer forests from Japan and eastern Siberia and from Alaska to California. This attractive little plant, whose generic name means "mayflower," bears a cluster of tiny white flowers.* (Stephen J. Krasemann/DRK Photo)

124 *overleaf. More than 140 inches of rain fall in one year on the forests of Washington's Olympic Peninsula, and the result is incredibly dense vegetation dominated by such towering trees as Douglas-fir, Sitka spruce (*Picea sitchensis*), and western hemlock (*Tsuga heterophylla*). The tree in the center of this scene, along the Hoh River, has been shattered by lightning. Fallen trees, quickly covered with soggy sphagnum, become nurse logs for the seedlings of the next generation of forest giants. In this rich environment, western sword ferns (*Polystichum munitum*) reach to a man's waist, and lichens, liverworts, and mosses abound.* (Harald Sund)

122 *and* **123.** *The showy "blossoms" of Pacific dogwood (*Cornus nuttalli*) are really six white bracts that encircle the cluster of true flowers. This handsome tree may reach a height of 50 feet in the Pacific rain forests. John James Audubon included Pacific dogwood in one of his paintings for* Birds of America, *and he named the tree for Thomas Nuttall, the eccentric botanist-explorer who first collected the plant.* (122 Steven C. Wilson/Entheos; 123 Keith Gunnar/Bruce Coleman, Inc.)

126. *A clump of redwood sorrel* (Oxalis oregana) *clings to a niche on the mossy trunk of a great Sitka spruce* (Picea sitchensis). *The heart-shaped leaflets of redwood sorrel often form lush carpets on the floor of cool forests from Washington to California. Its delicate flowers are white or pink, with purple veins.* (Tom and Pat Leeson)

127 *top. Little helmet mushrooms* (Mycena *sp.*)*, with dainty bell-shaped caps, grow on a rotting stump in Washington's Olympic rain forest. More than 230 species of* Mycena *mushrooms are found in North America, their caps tinted a wide range of colors—red, brown, yellow, orange, purple, white.* (Jim Brandenburg)

127 *bottom. The seed of a western hemlock* (Tsuga heterophylla) *germinated on this ancient stump, which is now encircled by the roots of the young tree. The grasping roots of an old, 200-foot-tall Sitka spruce* (Picea sitchensis) *in the background suggests a similar birth atop a mossy nurse log or stump.* (Steven C. Wilson/ Entheos)

128 *overleaf. Ferns, mosses, and a fungus known, because of its flavor, as chicken-of-the-woods* (Laetiporus sulphureus) *thrive on a toppled Douglas-fir* (Pseudotsuga menziesii) *in Alaska's Misty Fjords National Monument.* (Gary Braasch)

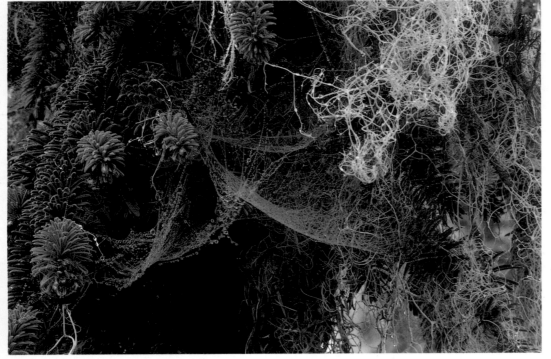

130 *top. Lichens and mist-soaked spider webs are draped from the branches of a Sitka spruce* (Picea sitchensis) *on Vancouver Island. Species of lichens, mosses, liverworts, and ferns number in the hundreds in Pacific Northwest rain forests.* (Steven C. Wilson/ Entheos)

130 *bottom left. Deer fern* (Blechnum spicant) *thrives on the moist forest floor of Washington's Kitsap Peninsula. A common fern in the cool coniferous forests of Eurasia and the Pacific Northwest, from Alaska to California, deer fern has two kinds of fronds: evergreen sterile fronds, and deciduous fertile fronds that arise from the center of the plant and stand dried and sere the following year.* (Steven C. Wilson/Entheos)

131. *Fresh leaves and flower buds emerge on a screen of shrubs at the edge of a Washington marsh. Early spring is a special time for visitors to forests in northern regions, for many trees and shrubs burst into varied and colorful bloom, while the forest floor is decorated by a profusion of wild-flowers.* (Steven C. Wilson/Entheos)

130 *above. A dense stand of Douglas-fir* (Pseudotsuga menziesii) *is reflected in the still waters of a pond in Glacier Bay National Park, Alaska. More lumber and plywood veneer is produced from Douglas-fir than from any other North American tree.* (Stephen J. Krasemann/ DRK Photo)

132, 133 and **134** overleaf. Dominant tree of the fog-enshrouded coastal forests of northern California is the majestic redwood (Sequoia sempervirens), *the tallest tree on Earth. A 368-foot specimen is the tallest surviving redwood, though it is likely that even larger trees fell to loggers' saws early in this century. Many small virgin groves of redwoods are protected in state parks, and one of the most bitterly fought conservation battles of recent years led to the creation of a Redwood National Park—but not before many of the finest areas in the proposed preserve were ravaged by lumber companies. Redwoods mature at 400 to 500 years, but trees more than 2,000 years old have been documented from annual growth rings on their stumps.* (Harald Sund)

136. *The bark of spotted gum* (Eucalyptus maculata), *one of more than 600 kinds of eucalyptus trees in Australia. So distinctive are the barks of various eucalypts that they are used as an identification guide. And the bark is so thick that it effectively protects the tree from scorching brushfires. Though flames may char the outer bark and burn the leaves, the inner bark and sapwood are protected and the tree will recover.* (Walter H. Hodge)

In the Land of Peppermint Gum: Australian Eucalypts

There is a eucalypt to suit every taste. If one takes that statement literally, there are lemon-scented gum (*Eucalyptus citriodora*), sugar gum (*E. cladocalyx*), and various peppermint gums. For travelers who set out to explore wild Australia, original home of these legendary eucalypts, there are landscapes to suit every taste, too, and a community of eucalypts to match nearly every type of terrain.

Descending into deep ravines, for example, we are engulfed by eucalypts and giant tree ferns (*Dicksonia* and *Cyathea*) as though we had entered a series of caverns. In these shadowed depths, protected from winds though not from rains, where the ecosystem has been stable for millennia, the trees have grown to great height. Even to record height.

Some years ago we chanced to read a book entitled *Forest Trees of Australia*, published by what was then the Forestry and Timber Bureau of the Commonwealth Government. In that book were the following statements: "Mountain ash (*Eucalyptus regnans*) of Victoria and Tasmania reaches heights of 320 feet, making it the tallest species in this country and the tallest hardwood in the world . . . Measurements of over 350 feet have been recorded."

How much over? Knowing that California redwoods reached a world-record height of 368 feet, we asked a biologist, soon after we arrived in Australia, where one could find such enormous eucalypts. The answer: "Mate, if there'd ever been trees that tall they would have been cut for lumber long ago." Even so, some massive examples of *E. regnans* remain, and they are without doubt among the world's most impressive trees.

If we go deeply enough into the ravine, the shadows erupt with loud and repetitious calls of the lyrebird, perhaps the most skillful of natural mimics. If we stay discreetly in the shadows, the bird will walk nonchalantly around us, all but ignoring us, singing steadily. Or it will ascend its carefully constructed mound of earth and throw the lyre-shaped mass of tail feathers over its head and down in front—a remarkable courtship display.

If we climb a mountain slope, we may do so by starting up a thickly vegetated ravine, as up Mount Mitchell, in Cunningham Gap National Park, Queensland. After about a mile through dense, moist alcove forest, protected from wind, we round a bend and immediately enter open hillside eucalypt woods and patches of grass trees (*Xanthorrhoea*), a member of the lily family. These ungainly tipped and tilted trees look like something out of the Permian Period, but everywhere they are dominated by stately eucalypts that cover so many of the mountain ranges of Australia.

Other contrasts in eucalypt communities often strike us unexpectedly. On the ridges in Lamington National Park, Queensland, the spreading trees shelter pied currawongs, abundant, noisy black-and-white birds that fill the woods with wailing sounds. A moment later, the epitome of beauty, a rainbow lorikeet flies past. A parrot of red, blue, green, yellow, and orange feathers, it is one of the continent's most colorful birds.

Eucalypts even tolerate the snow—what there is of it in Australia. On the peaks of Kosciusko National Park, snow gums (*Eucalyptus pauciflora* var. *alpina*) preside over the broad snowfields of July and host flocks of crimson rosella, a wide-ranging parrot with scarlet and lavender plumage so vivid it never fails to astonish us.

Another landscape is that of the hilly country west of Sydney. En route to hike in canyons of Blue Mountains National Park, we came to what looked like marching legions of ghosts. But they were only the crooked white boles of scribbly gum. On the trunk of this tree the scribbly gum moths lay their eggs between the bark of the old season and the bark of the new. Later, the larvae burrow between these layers and leave tunnels which are revealed as grooves when the old bark falls away.

Proceeding west of the mountains, we discover that the landscape of inland Australia becomes more prairielike and the trees take on a character far different from that of the ravines or ridges or rain forests. But the semiarid prairies and rolling hills are, in places, covered with a eucalypt community called the mallee. Here no tall or towering trees with single trunks stand out as guideposts for the wilderness traveler. The forest becomes far less majestic than that dominated by *Eucalyptus regnans;* the trees have multiple trunks, especially the ubiquitous yellow mallee (*E. incrassata*). The tree is not very tall; the average height is 12 feet. Nor does the woodland vary much in appearance. The forest floor is strewn with gray disintegrating bark that has peeled from the tree trunks. A few inconspicuous shrubs, *Leptospermum* among them, flower in September. The porcupine grass (*Triodia irritans*) grows first as a single clump, then outward in circular rings as the center dies. Such is the mallee forest. Lacking landmarks and variations, its sameness may mislead the traveler unless he follows a trail or a compass needle.

Nevertheless, the mallee offers surprises. The eucalypt with all its oils is a highly flammable tree and we may come across miles of sandy plain once burnt free of vegetation. In such situations, forests of *Banksia* burgeon, producing hard-shelled seeds that few but the yellow-tailed black cockatoos, with very strong beaks, can open. In the absence of further fires, the eucalypts may dominate again, but such succession is slow in drought-prone lands. Another surprise in mallee woods is the mallee fowl, the best-known mound-building bird of Australia.

There is hardly any end when we delve into a study of eucalypts; they comprise about 95 percent of Australian forests and there are approximately 600 species of them. Some hybridize readily, further complicating matters. The family Myrtaceae, to which the genus *Eucalyptus* belongs, is of fairly recent origin. Since species within its genera have not yet become rigidly separated, they often interbreed, principally because pollen grains can easily be transferred from one species to another.

Many eucalypts have only a tiny range, and are thus

highly specialized. Some have showy flowers, even though the petals are fused and drop early. The stamens may be so colorful and abundant that they take the place of showy petals. Before the flowers open they are covered by an operculum, or cap. From this the trees get their name: *eu* meaning "well" and *kalyptos* meaning "covered."

There are many other names, both aboriginal and historic, for eucalypts, including wandoo, marri, ghost, illyarrie, woollybutt, messmate, yorrel, and mugga. The coolabah (*Eucalyptus microtheca*) figures in the opening of A. B. Paterson's celebrated poem "Waltzing Matilda": "Oh! there once was a swagman camped in a Billabong / Under the shade of a Coolabah tree . . ." In aboriginal legend, the mystique of the gum tree is engraved in Koobor's tale, the koala-boy who got all he needed to drink from the leaves of the tree but could, if he wanted, cause such a severe drought that everyone except koalas would die of thirst. Australia's film master-piece, the mystic and mysterious *Picnic at Hanging Rock*, portrays an ill-fated outing in a eucalypt grove.

As for animals, few are so species-specific in their eating habits as the shy and retiring koala, a representative of Australia's marsupialian fauna; of the hundreds of types of eucalypts available, koalas eat the leaves of only perhaps a dozen. And there is enough moisture in this diet so that the animals need never descend for water (the aboriginal name for them, *koolah*, means "no drink").

Kangaroos, emus, and galahs may be seen feeding in wild swamps or in open woodlands and prairies. Where there are ants there are echidnas, small mammalian predators, also called spiny anteaters. Remarkably brilliant birds, such as sulfur-crested cockatoos, red-backed parrots, blue wrens, and red-capped robins enliven the mallee forest. High up in the branches of river red gums (*Eucalyptus camaldulensis*) may be found nests of wedge-tailed eagles and peregrine falcons.

In due course, orchids spring up on the forest floor, kangaroos hop in to feed on ondoroo plants (*Solanum simile*), and the eagles return to nest. The eucalypt forest burgeons once more, unconquerable and incomparable.

141. *A forest of manna gum* (Eucalyptus viminalis) *reaches skyward in New South Wales. Manna gum, which grows to a height of 120 feet on Australia's east coast and in Tasmania, is named for a sugary substance exuded by the bark and leaves. The "manna" piles up at the base of the tree and is gathered as food by insects.* (Jean-Paul Ferrero)

142 *top left. Dead and dying eucalypts provide roosting and nesting hollows for many kinds of animals that, in turn, cross-pollinate the eucalyptus flowers and help maintain the genetic vitality of the forest.*
(Kjell B. Sandved)

142 *top right. A towering manna gum* (Eucalyptus viminalis) *is draped with ribbons of shed bark. Though the eucalypts include the tallest hardwoods in the world, they are not particularly long-lived trees, for their wood is vulnerable to attack by termites and fungi. A 300-foot mountain ash* (Eucalyptus regnans) *may collapse at an age of 400 years. A few species with more durable wood may live for 1,000 years.*
(Kjell B. Sandved)

143. *Hieroglyphics on the bark of a scribbly gum* (Eucalyptus mannifera) *are the tunnels of bark-boring moth larvae. Only six species of eucalypts grow beyond the Australian shores, and of those only one is not also native to the island continent.*
(Walter H. Hodge)

142 *above. A snow gum* (Eucalyptus niphophila) *has been twisted by fierce winds high on Mount Kosciusko, Australia's highest peak. Where they are sheltered from gales that reach hurricane force, these broad-leaved evergreen trees grow at altitudes of as much as 6,500 feet.*
(Stanley Breeden)

142 *above. A white gum* (Eucalyptus alba) *has shed most of its old bark, revealing a fresh layer of smooth, orange-red bark that will eventually bleach to the tree's characteristic color. Gums shed their bark annually, usually at the height of summer.*
(Stanley Breeden)

144 and **145** *top. Eucalyptus flowers develop within a bud, capped by an operculum, formed by fused petals. The operculum may hang from the tree for several weeks before it splits open and a mass of bright-colored stamens unfolds, each filament capped with pollen. A tree of the West Australian sandplain known as the mottlecah* (Eucalyptus macrocarpa) *has the largest flowers of its kind, up to 3 inches across.* (Walter H. Hodge)

145 *bottom. Darwin woollybutt* (Eucalyptus miniata) *grows widely on Australia's north coast. Mottlecah and woollybutt are just two of numerous colloquial names, many of aboriginal origin, for eucalypts. The caps of eucalypt flowers vary widely in shape and color, but the stamens are limited to warm tones—reds, oranges, yellows—and creamy whites.* (Stanley Breeden)

146 *overleaf. Of Australia's many marsupial animals, only kangaroos, wallabies, and the famous koala* (Phascolarctos cinereus) *are active in daylight. The koala, whose scientific name means "pouched bear," feeds exclusively on the oily leaves of a dozen species of of eucalypts—leaves that are poisonous to other animals. An adult koala, weighing about 30 pounds, will consume 2-1/2 pounds of eucalyptus leaves each day. Symbiotic bacteria that live in the koala's extra-long intestines detoxify the leaves.* (Alan Foley/Bruce Coleman, Ltd.)

148. *A stand of poplars* (Populus sp.) *thrive in a Holland marsh. Like the closely related willows* (Salix), *poplars are commonly found in moist areas—on stream banks or the borders of lakes and swamps—because their tiny seeds sprout only on damp, bare ground. Some 35 species of poplars occur in the Northern Hemisphere.* (Kees Van Den Berg/N.A.S./Photo Researchers, Inc.)

Deciduous Woodlands: Celebration of the Seasons

General William Booth, founder of the Salvation Army, once said that nothing moves people like the terrific. "They must have hell-fire flashed before their faces," he said, "or they will not move."

Volcanoes move them, especially glowing fountains of lava that erupt 2,000 feet into the air. Great waterfalls move them, like Iguazú, in Argentina, where 278 cataracts pour forth with a thunderous roar. The Grand Canyon moves them. Coral reefs of the South Pacific Ocean move them. The wildflower displays of Western Australia move them.

Of trees, alas, none bursts into fountains of lava. And not one roars like a waterfall. For most of their lives their effect is discreet and subtle. But the seasons advance to a climax. In winter the temperate forest raises naked arms above the snow. With the first warm days, a host of plants on the forest floor begin to bloom. In spring, some trees, such as southern catalpa (*Catalpa bignonioides*), give birth to masses of flowers. In summer, the woods repose in rich green foliage, producing nuts and nectar and fruits. But the grandest spectacle of all is incomparable. It moves a million people every year, or two million or three, to their cameras, into their vehicles, out on the trail. It has no roar, little movement, and absolutely no advice from human beings. It is the changing color of autumn leaves in the North American deciduous forest.

True, there are notable displays of fall foliage in deciduous woods of China, Japan, Europe, and South America. But in North America this massive coloring occurs from coast to coast and from Canada to Mexico, more than a million square miles of landscape converted to such pervasive colors that they move people like little else.

The event is forecast on a long-range basis, predicted from day to day, advertised, announced in newspapers, broadcast on radio, and filmed for television. Tourists journey thousands of miles to witness the spectacle. One sunny Sunday, October 12, 1975, during the peak of the season, 52,591 cars moved bumper to bumper along the Skyline Drive in Shenandoah National Park, Virginia. The 500-mile-long Blue Ridge Parkway in Virginia and North Carolina receives some 16 million visitors a year, not the least for autumn views from mountain overlooks. Spectacle is big business, and it seems safe to question whether any aspect of wild living trees attracts more attention or benefits more human economies than the coming of autumn color.

In North America, at least, it is hard to think of certain localities—eastern Canada, New England, the Great Smoky Mountains, the Ozarks—without depicting them in the reds and yellows and oranges of their autumn leaves. For the world's greatest concentration of deciduous forest lies in these areas, especially along the Appalachian Mountain chain between Alabama and Maine. Moreover, the tree with possibly the widest distribution in North America, the quaking aspen (*Populus tremuloides*), has become world-renowned for its spectacular coloration. And where there are no forests, where only cottonwoods follow river courses across the prairies and in the arid West, the changing colors can be striking. It isn't hell-fire but it moves people on a grander, more systematic basis than perhaps any other natural living phenomenon.

Were it not for the pigments in these leaves and the way they are revealed, the forest would be more like those in the tropics, where deciduous leaves fall inconspicuously, one at a time, seldom turning color. Here in the temperate zone the process begins when a disk of cells near the base of the leaf stem starts to turn to cork. This abscission layer slowly grows across the stem, choking off the flow of nutrients and water to the leaf. Since that interrupts the production of green chlorophyll, the leaf begins to die. As the green fades, it no longer masks the other colors in the leaf—xanthophyll (bright yellow), carotene (yellow-orange), anthocyanin (red and purple).

Many observers claim that the star performer in this spectacle is the sugar maple (*Acer saccharum*), whose leaves are big enough and bright enough to stand out for miles, often dominating the northeastern quadrant of the United States and eastern Canada. The maples, indeed, account for a major share of the continent's autumn color, from the red maple (*A. rubrum*), even wider in distribution than the sugar maple, to the vivid bigtooth maple (*A. grandidentatum*) of western mountains, to the vine maple (*A. circinatum*) of the Pacific Northwest.

There are nearly four times as many species of oaks as maples in North America, but only a few compare in the brilliance of their fall foliage. Chief among them are the red oak (*Quercus rubra*) and the scarlet oak (*Q. coccinea*). Seldom does any single species of tree dominate in the forests of the southern Appalachians, and the visitor soon becomes confused (albeit impressed) by the multiple colors in a densely wooded valley. But old-timers in these parts can readily identify the trees from afar by subtle differences in their hues. The large leaves of yellow poplar (*Liriodendron tulipifera*), also called tulip tree from the shape of its flowers, turn bright yellow. Sassafras (*Sassafras albidum*) becomes a cinnamon orange, dogwood (*Cornus florida*) a dark red, and sweet gum (*Liquidambar styraciflua*) a reddish purple.

For millions of years, the southern Appalachians have been in ecologic repose, especially in protected mountain coves where the deciduous forest reaches its most impressive development. With mild winters and hot summers where rainfall measures 70 inches a year at moderate elevations, well over a hundred species of trees crowd together in the valleys and coves of the Southern Highlands. That will not seem like many species to the connoisseur of tropical forests, where hundreds of species abound. But it is close to a record for temperate forests.

Inside, the virgin deciduous forest seems almost like the interior of a cathedral. Broad leaves of hickory (*Carya*) interlock overhead and filter the sunlight as though through a stained-glass window. Great cathedral-like columns are provided by a member of the magnolia family, the yellow poplar, whose straight gray trunks rise up and disappear among the leaves. So conducive are these Appalachian vales to growth and survival that a number of North American trees reach their greatest height here. A yellow buckeye (*Aesculus octandra*), for example, attains a circumference of 16 feet. Red squirrels consume great quantities of the buckeye's glossy fruits.

As we move among the contorted roots and fallen trunks on the forest floor we are soon surrounded by numerous species: red oak, black cherry, yellow buckeye, sugar maple, red maple, hickory, black locust, silverbell, basswood. Many are huge and mature, a rarity in forested regions where the lumberjack prevails.

Suddenly we hear a loud snap, as though of a rifle crack. An acorn has plummeted from the branch of a red oak and landed on the forest floor. It won't last long, what with all the squirrels and bears and wild turkeys around. The multiple and intricate facets of deciduous woodlands are certainly more than we can absorb and contemplate on a single excursion. And every time we repeat this trek there will be fresh discoveries. As the American naturalist John Burroughs said: "To find new things, take the path you took yesterday."

We encounter the unexpected green of hemlock (*Tsuga*). And there are still flowers around, even after the leaves have fallen: the odd one out, the witch hazel (*Hamamelis virginiana*), sends out its slender yellow petals just as the sharpened winds of winter filter through the forest.

A massive basswood (*Tilia*) long ago died and crashed to the forest floor. Under steady attack by invertebrate animals, as well as bacteria and fungi, it has begun to disintegrate. Already part of it has crumbled to dark brown dust, a natural fertilizer that helps assure the growth of future generations of herbs, shrubs, and trees—and the animals dependent upon them.

If General Booth was right, and people are moved by the terrific, then for generations to come there are likely to be large sanctuaries where these colorful trees can go on living in their natural state. And as reliably as the earth swings on its orbit, and the tourists arrive, and the bears fatten for winter, the deciduous forest will every autumn produce a spectacle like no other on earth.

153. *An American elm* (Ulmus americana) *in fresh spring foliage. A beloved shade tree across eastern North America, the vase-shaped elm has been devastated by Dutch elm disease, a fungus spread by beetles tunneling beneath the bark. Over the last half-century, the blight—which attacks the tree's tissue, blocks the water flow, and causes branches to wilt and die—has killed countless millions of stately elms. Spraying the trees with toxic chemicals to kill the beetles not only failed to control the disease, it decimated songbird populations.* (John deVisser)

154 *overleaf. An oak spinney sprawls across the landscape in rural Sussex, England. "Spinney" is a British word for a small wood, or grove of trees. England's oak forests were ravaged during the age of wooden ships, when 2,000 large trees were used to build one 72-gun warship. In 1810, it took five men twenty days to cut down a 400-year-old oak, and two sawyers spent another five months converting it to boards. Lesser oaks were stripped of their bark for tanning leather; the used bark was spread on streets to deaden the noise of carriage wheels and horses' hooves near houses where people lay ill. Surprisingly, noted oak woods still survive in almost every county of England, Wales, Scotland, and Ireland.* (Su Gooders/Ardea)

156 *top. A grove of bur oaks* (Quercus macrocarpa) *flank a prairie river in Minnesota. This tree, a pioneer species in Midwestern grasslands, also is called the mossycup oak because of the pointed scales that fringe its acorns. These large nuts are an important food supply for many animals, especially the colorful wood ducks that inhabit bottomland forests.* (Jim Brandenburg)

156 *bottom. On a mountainside in Colorado, quaking aspens* (Populus tremuloides) *unveil their new greenery. No other North American tree has so wide a distribution as the quaking aspen, which grows from Alaska to Labrador and southward along the Rocky Mountains into Mexico. Its popular and scientific names refer to the leaves, which quaver in the lightest breeze.* (Jonathan T. Wright)

157. *Ranks of tuliptrees* (Liriodendron tulipifera) *march up the side of Clingman's Dome in the Great Smoky Mountains of Tennessee. Named for its huge, greenish-yellow flowers, the tuliptree grows tall and straight, its first branches 80 to 100 feet above the ground. The massive trunks once were used as masts for sailing ships.* (Larry West/ Bruce Coleman, Inc.)

158. *Six to 8 inches wide, the creamy-white flowers of southern magnolia* (Magnolia grandiflora) *perfume forests of the coastal plain from North Carolina to Texas. One noted authority called this evergreen species, which may attain a height of 100 feet, "the most splendid ornamental tree in the American forests." The flowering season covers more than a month, and individual blossoms last up to 4 days.*
(Jack Dermid)

159 *top. None of the shrubs and trees that lure springtime travelers to the mountains of eastern North America have blossoms more beautiful than flame azalea* (Rhododendron calendulaceum), *whose clustered flowers range in color from orange to scarlet. Long pollen-bearing stamens protrude from the mouth of each vaselike flower.*
(Jack Dermid)

159 *bottom. The true flowers of flowering dogwood* (Cornus florida) *are tiny and inconspicuous, crowded into a head less than one inch across. They are surrounded by showy, petal-like bracts that traditionally are snow-white, but in some cultivated varieties are shocking pink.*
(Nicholas F. Delagi)

160 *overleaf. Spring is in full swing in the hardwood forests of the Great Smokies in this view from a mountaintop. Some 100 species of trees and 1,300 kinds of flowering plants have been catalogued in the Great Smoky Mountains, where much of the forest is virgin—untouched by an ax since the first colonists arrived from Europe.*
(Sonja Bullaty/Angelo Lomeo)

162. *Yellow birches* (Betula alleghaniensis) *shade Moss Glen Falls in a Vermont wilderness preserve. A tree of moist forests at lower elevations, yellow birch may live for 200 years—a ripe old age for any member of the birch family. And it is the most important species of birch economically, its close-grained wood used for veneers, tool handles, and snow-shoe frames.* (Richard W. Brown)

163 *top left. Large-flowered trilliums* (Trillium grandiflorum) *bloom in the rich soil of an Appalachian woodland, where a fallen American chestnut* (Castanea dentata) *slowly decays. Once one of the New World's most valuable trees—for its indestructible wood, edible nuts, and tannin—the American chestnut was decimated by an introduced blight that began its deadly rampage around 1904. Only a handful of mature trees, apparently immune to the fungus, still survive, although sprouts continue to grow from the stumps of ancient trees.*
(James P. Valentine)

163 *top right. Fog swirls about a grove of oaks* (Quercus sp.) *in the Great Smoky Mountains, where more than 500,000 acres are protected as a national park. Flowers of sneezeweed* (Helenium autumnale), *with their down-turned rays, glow in the muted light.* (Sonja Bullaty/Angelo Lomeo)

163 *bottom. Summer wildflowers— ox-eye daisies* (Chrysanthemum leucanthemum) *and orange hawk-weed* (Hieracium aurantiacum)— *carpet a meadow in the Great Smoky Mountains. Like so many other North American wildflowers, both are aliens, introduced from Europe either accidentally or intentionally by early settlers. In the background is a mature stand of paper birch* (Betula papyrifera). (Richard W. Brown)

165. *Both the foliage and nuts of Ohio buckeye (*Aesculus glabra) *are poisonous, and the twigs and leaflets, if crushed, give off a foul odor. But early settlers took these characteristics as a sign that the tree had great medicinal powers, and they carried buckeye seeds in their pockets to ward off rheumatism. A close relative of the horse-chestnut of Europe, this is the official state tree of Ohio.* (John Shaw)

166 *overleaf. An autumn storm approaches a Michigan forest, where maples and oaks have donned bright fall colors but a cluster of quaking aspens (*Populus tremuloides) *has not yet turned its characteristic gold.* (John Shaw)

164 *above. Yellowish-green flowers droop from a branchlet of striped maple (*Acer pensylvanicum)*, a shrub or small tree of the understory in cool Northeastern forests. This species is also called "moosewood" because moose, as well as deer and beaver, eat its smooth, striped bark.* (Walter H. Hodge)

164 *top left. New leaves form on a branchlet of a red maple (*Acer rubrum)*, a very common tree in the woodlands of eastern North America. Equally at home in up- land or swampy situations, red maple has bright red flowers in spring and scarlet leaves in autumn. Its bark yielded ink and dyes for pioneer families.* (David Overcash/ Bruce Coleman, Inc.)

164 *top right. A paper birch seedling (*Betula papyrifera) *sprouts from a bed of haircap moss on the Michigan shore of Lake Superior. Pure stands of birch are found in such cool, wet locales, though the tree usually grows mixed with a wide assortment of hardwoods and conifers.* (John Shaw)

168, 169 *and* **170** *overleaf. In late September and early October, autumn overtakes the mixed deciduous forests of the north-eastern United States, painting the foliage with a palette of warm hues ranging from crimson to old gold. Millions of people make weekend excursions into wooded rural areas to view and photograph the spectacular, if too brief, display of fall colors; and experienced woodsmen can identify many trees at a glance simply by their leaf colors, which are masked during spring and summer months by green chlorophyll. (168 Robert P. Carr; 169 John Shaw; 170-171 Richard W. Brown)*

172 and **173.** *Trees of the maple genus* Acer *alone show virtually all of the color shades to be found in the autumn forest. Thirteen of the 200 species of maples are native to North America, and several other kinds have been introduced from Europe and Asia as shade trees or ornamentals. The maple leaf is the national emblem of* Canada, *and the strong wood of many maples is used for furniture, cabinet-making, veneers, and flooring. In late winter, when trees once again stir to life, the sugar maple (Acer saccharum) is tapped for its sweet sap, which is boiled and concentrated to produce maple syrup and sugar candies. A venerable, majestic sugar maple may yield 60 gallons of sap a year, which will produce about 1 gallon of syrup or 4½ pounds of sugar. Sugaring operations range from tapping a few trees for home consumption to a major industry in Canada that sells millions of bottles of syrup.* (172 top Richard Rowan; 172 bottom and 173 John Eastcott/Yva Momatiuk)

174 *overleaf. An abandoned orchard in New England, with apple trees* (Malus sylvestris) *that were planted near the turn of the century, is overgrown with shining sumac* (Rhus copallina). *Many apple varieties that once were famous for their wonderful flavors and textures are no longer grown commercially. They have been replaced on the market by genetically engineered apples that are easy to grow, ship, and store — but are hard-skinned and largely tasteless. As is so often the case with modern agriculture, the grower benefits and the consumer is unaware of the heritage that has been lost. But those old-time apples still ripen on forgotten trees such as these, and they feed sweet-toothed deer when they fall into the weeds below.* (Robert P. Carr)

176. *The forest floor in a nearly pure stand of sugar maples* (Acer saccharum), *in northern Michigan, is crowded with seedlings awaiting their turn in the sun. If an old tree should fall—and a sugar maple may live for 250 years—a seedling will quickly fill the gap, growing rapidly during its first 40 years of life. A single mature maple will produce thousands of two-winged fruits each year. Most are eaten by birds and small animals; only a handful will germinate to populate the understory nursery.*
(John Shaw)

177. *An autumn crocus* (Crocus nudiflorus) *blooms in the leaf litter of a forest in France. Leaves of the autumn crocus appear in spring*

and die before the purple flowers emerge in September and October.
(Harold Davis)

178 *overleaf. Colorful bracket fungi* (Polyporus sulphureus) *thrive on a rotting log in an Ontario woodland. Dying and dead trees are a vital part of a healthy forest ecosystem. They not only host such forms of life as fungi, which break down organic matter, but they provide homes and habitat for a wide range of animal life—birds, mammals, insects, amphibians, and such creatures as millipedes.*
(Carroll W. Perkins)

180 and **181.** *A fresh snowfall blankets a Vermont woodlot. Very little of the original forest was left uncut by early generations of New Englanders. But where farming proved uneconomical and fields were abandoned, the land was quickly reclaimed by the trees. Present-day threats to the new Yankee Forest include the rapid spread of land-consuming second-home developments, and the growing demand for trees to fuel not only wood-burning stoves but giant wood-fired power plants that will generate megawatts of electricity.* (Richard W. Brown)

182 *overleaf. A winter moon rises over a leafless white ash (*Fraxinus americana*) in northern Michigan. Many deciduous trees can be recognized in winter by their distinctive silhouettes—especially trees growing alone in fields and pastures where branches can develop their characteristic shapes. The wood of white ash is in great demand for making sports equipment: baseball bats, hockey sticks, tennis racquets, and oars and paddles.* (John Shaw)

184. *Fir needles* (Abies *sp.) are scattered over old snow in the Wenatchee National Forest of eastern Washington. Trees of the northern hemisphere, some 40 species of firs occur in cold and temperate regions around the world. Steep, high mountain slopes may be robed in pure stands of fir. These are important timber trees, but firs also are vital to wildlife for both food and shelter.*
(Ed Cooper)

Of Lakes and Loons: The Boreal Forest

On the second day out we break camp and take to our canoes again, but we are not in them for long. There is no better way to find out how glaciers disrupted drainage patterns in the north woods than to get repeatedly out of your canoe and pack around six or seven portages, as must be done on the way to Lower Basswood Falls. It is a watery Canadian wilderness, and Canada boasts the largest lake and conifer environment in North America.

Third day. From Lower Basswood Falls we paddle north across Tuck Lake and via Tuck River to Robinson Lake. There have been no motors to mar the music of rippling waters and singing sparrows. We leave no trail, and follow none. The farther we go, the more cognizant we become of the woods as fountains of life.

The North American boreal coniferous forest, one of the world's largest forests, stretches 4,000 miles from Labrador to Alaska, and south along Appalachian Mountain ridges to Tennessee. Although they are subject to extreme winter weather conditions and to infestations of insects that devastate whole tracts, these woods have managed to evolve and adapt and, over the millennia, develop rich ecosystems.

Three pines dominate: red (*Pinus resinosa*), a handsome shapely species that may grow to 100 feet in height; eastern white (*P. strobus*), largest of the northeastern conifers; and jack (*P. banksiana*), a ragged type that can grow on relatively poor soils and is usually the first to spring up following a fire. In the west and north, great plateaus, mountain

This was the country for Paul. Trees and trees and trees. Pines and maples and oaks for thousands of miles, from the Great Lakes clear through the Northwest right out to the Pacific Ocean. Here were trees so wide you'd get tired walking around their trunks, trees so high it took an ordinary man a whole week to see to the top of them.
—Louis Untermeyer,
The Wonderful Adventures of Paul Bunyan

185

ranges, and flatlands are occupied by uniform and nearly pure stands of lodgepole pine (*P. contorta*). Beneath these may be nearly endless miles of fire-weed, or glades of bluebells, or fields of wild geraniums and larkspurs.

The boreal forest typically has two other major conifers, the black and white spruces. The lesser of these is the black (*Picea mariana*), often found in cold swamps, where it may be extremely slow-growing: trees 2 inches in diameter have been found to be more than 120 years old. The white spruce (*P. glauca*), given good growing conditions, reaches 100 feet in height and a diameter of 2 feet.

As we cruise along the rivers and at the edges of lakes, we see that the wall of woods confronting us is by no means all coniferous or dark and gloomy. Stands of white-barked quaking aspen (*Populus tremuloides*) mingle with the needled trees, holding their own until crowded out in the natural succession of forest life. In wetter places the paper birch (*Betula papyrifera*), a common Canadian species, sinks its roots into the shallow sandy loam. Sometimes we launch our canoes in a mucklike muddy "soup," which seems unusual in a region of pure clean lakes and crystal waters. But this only reminds us that some lakes, in nature's endless state of transition, are dying. A steady accumulation of needles, leaves, and debris falls into them, decays, and turns to mud, producing a bog, then soil and meadow.

In the final stages of shallow water, a growth of aquatic plants—spatterdock, water lily, pondweed, sedge—takes over. With this, the muskrats, beavers, and otters move in. Alders begin to grow. They attract sparrows and redstarts. As the water evaporates and the soil becomes less damp, aquatic plants are crowded out by mosses, ferns, wild rice, and such shrubs as blueberry (*Vaccinium*). Minks make their homes in chambers of sphagnum moss. Where the warmth and light of the sun circulate, a patch of willows (or cedars or ash) may hold brief hegemony, until at last the spruce and pine edge in and produce the climax forest. If we hike out of the swamps onto granite uplands where the soil is well drained, we come to stands of scrub oak (*Quercus*).

Fourth day. Mile after mile we paddle deeper into the wilderness, still lost in a maze of lakes. Mosquitoes, flies, and midges make life in these woods unpleasant sometimes, but we have no desire to flee. We did not come here to rough it; as Old Nessmuk (George Washington Sears) said, we came here to smooth it. Things are rough enough back in the civilized world, midges or no midges. We see few wild animals, other than birds, and conclude that the furbearing species whose pelts were so often sought by the *voyageurs* are either less abundant than a century ago or merely less obvious. Certainly the wolves are less conspicuous; we do not see or hear a one in the ten days we are here. Yet they are there, and in winter their specific routes are well defined. We do see deer, which seem out of place in woods so dense. And we pass some moose, standing in water near willows. Beaver lodges we notice quite often, as well as inconspicuous trails attributed to otters or muskrats. We may also find woodland caribou; they thrive in climax forests such as this.

Fifth and sixth days. North to Brent Lake and an island on which we camp for two nights. The early mornings are calm, the shoreline trees enveloped in a drifting mist. But by midday the wind has blown the fog away. Clouds race in over the tips of the spruce, and a squall of rain blurs the trees. Although precipitation falls rather uniformly through the year, there are times, especially in autumn, when the woods dry out. If a lightning storm should strike at such a time, it could set off fires that would wipe out large tracts of the boreal forest. But nature rekindles the life of burned-out places in somewhat the same way that it converts a bog from open space to wooded land.

Seventh day. Backtracking to McIntyre Lake and negotiating a short portage eastward, we pass numerous islands and wooded ridges, then make camp on the shore of Sarah Lake. No sooner do we open up our supplies and begin to prepare dinner than the Canada jays come swooping in to pilfer what we dare to leave unattended.

Eighth day. We turn south, feeling more at home in these north woods as the days pass. The air is a little cooler now, reminder of how short the summers are. September and October will be the best months— the air sharp and clear, the insects fewer.

Ninth day. We make our way south again, over long portages, and camp on the shore of Kett Lake, tired and ready for bed before the last of the daylight disappears. We hear the call of the loons again, one answering another across the lake.

Tenth day. Long paddles and portages back to Basswood Lake leave us with a feeling of having negotiated miles of inland waterways through huge expanses of trees. Yet we have entered only a corner of the boreal forest. Travel on, and we could go for days, months, years, without exploring all of the rest of it. And if for some reason all this was not enough to satisfy our wanderlust, extensive coniferous forests spread across the northern regions of Europe and Asia. And they have the same salutary effect on travelers. Alfred Nobel, the nineteenth-century Swedish inventor, said: "I want to live among trees and bushes, silent friends who respect the state of my nerves."

In Europe, however, some of the occupants are different; in those forests of spruce (*Picea*) and pine (*Pinus*) one hears the wailing cry of black-throated divers rather than loons. The capercaillie, largest of grouse, feeds in the pine forest and there performs its strutting, trancelike ritual dance. And if one explores deeply enough into the woods, a number of animals counterpart to those in North America may be found: bison, deer, elk, bear, wolverine.

When the paddler beaches his canoe for the last time on this trip and walks away from it, he is likely to have a nostalgic virus that will survive winter, civilization, and time. The boreal forest seems synonymous with paradise, a place where there are no heat waves, no droughts, no hurricanes. Only lakes and roaring streams and wildflowers and canoes and backpacks. And the pervading fragrance of pine and spruce. "While man might unravel the puzzled skein of life and solve the riddles of the universe," wrote Sigurd Olson, naturalist of the north woods, in *Runes of the North*, "what really matters is the wonder which makes it all possible. Back of everything is always a net of dreams."

189. *Paper birch* (Betula papyrifera), *young and old, stand side-by-side against winter winds along the Kobuk River of northern Alaska. This familiar tree of the northern United States and Canada is famous for the canoes made by North American Indians, who stretched the tree's tough bark over a cedar frame, then sealed the stitches with pine resin.* (Steven C. Wilson/ Entheos)

190 *overleaf. A forest of black spruce* (Picea mariana) *in northern British Columbia. Black spruce cones may remain open on the trees for several years until the heat of a forest fire stimulates them to shed their seeds. But the trees can also reproduce by a method called "layering": lower branches that become lightly covered by forest litter or soil develop roots that send up new shoots.* (Fred Bruemmer)

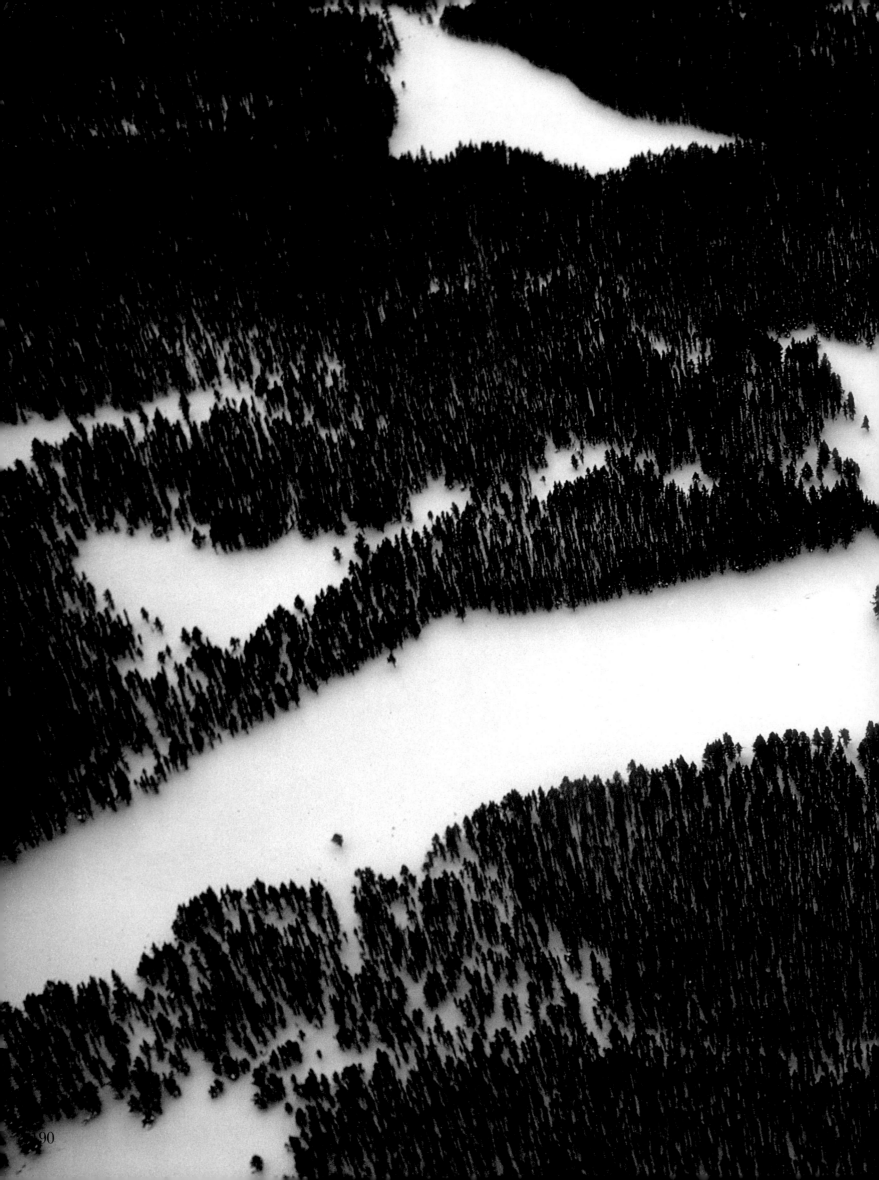

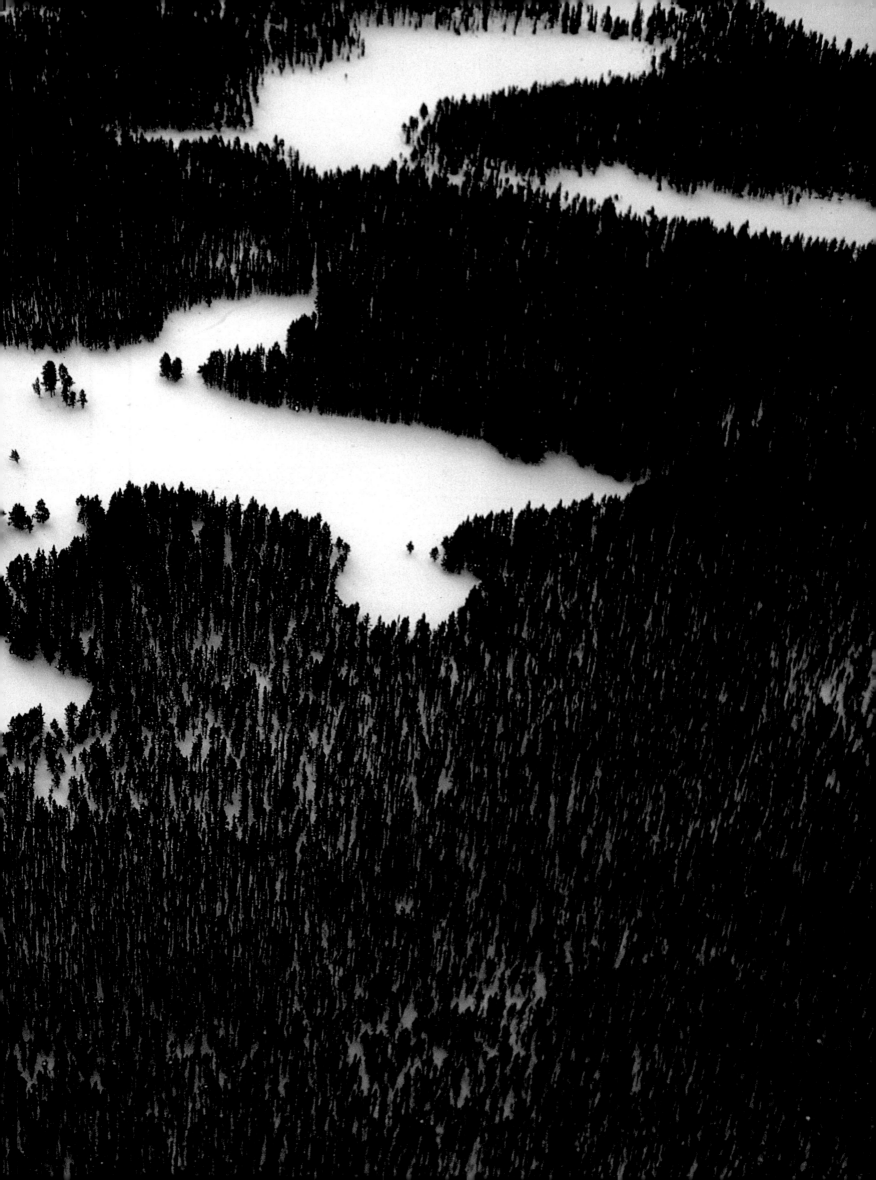

192. *A bald eagle* (Haliaeetus leucocephalus) *leaves its lofty perch in a spruce* (Picea sp.) *on the shore of Alaska's Lake Clark. This area is among many spectacular wilderness preserves, totaling more than 100 million acres, that are protected as national parks, wildlife refuges, and wild rivers under legislation passed by the U.S. Congress in 1980.* (Jim Brandenburg)

193. *A dead snag is the home for a boreal owl* (Aegolius funereus), *a raptor of northern coniferous forests around the world. Old pileated woodpecker holes are this night hunter's favorite nesting places. The boreal owl is so tame, and so inactive by day—when it*

remains hidden in dense foliage— that Eskimos easily catch it by hand. (Jim Brandenburg)

194 *overleaf. Mount Hunter, elevation 14,573 feet, looms over Kahiltna Glacier in Alaska's Mount McKinley National Park. In the foreground, columns of spruce trees* (Picea sp.) *catch the low sunlight. A century-old spruce in south- eastern Alaska may stand 100 feet high; but one that old in northern Alaska's Brooks Range may reach only 20 feet because of its harsh environment.* (Joe Rychetnik/N.A.S./Photo Researchers, Inc.)

196. *Fresh and faded cones layer the ground under a nearly pure stand of lodgepole pines (Pinus contorta)* in California's Sierra Nevada wilderness. American Indians used this abundant tree, which grows from Alaska to Baja California, to erect their tepees, hence the name lodgepole pine. Over its broad range, the lodgepole pine is found from sea level to elevations of 11,500 feet. Trees along the coast and in northern boglands tend to be stunted and twisted, a fact reflected in the specific name, *contorta, and in such local names as "screw pine."* (David Muench)

Cold Forests: Trees of Mountain and Tundra

Because they are among the hardiest and best
adapted of living organisms, trees have a remarkable
"staying power." Unable to move, they have had to
withstand fire, flood, storm, drought, and cold. Whole
groves may die under insect attack, yet individual
trees survive to repopulate. Through a remarkable
array of adaptations developed over hundreds of
millions of years, trees can resist cold and drought,
spring back after fire, avoid the loss of fluids, and
keep from being eaten. The tallest, oldest, and largest
living organisms on earth are trees.

Paradoxically, the oldest and largest of trees grow
in some of the coldest mountain climates. The
General Sherman Tree, one of the giant sequoias
(*Sequoiadendron giganteum*), grows at an elevation
of 7,000 feet above sea level in the Sierra Nevada of
California. It measures 272.4 feet in height, 36 feet
in diameter at the base, and contains an estimated
50,010 cubic feet of wood, the greatest bulk of any
living object. Obviously, all the snow and cold and
occasional forest fires of the last 3,500 years during
which this tree is estimated to have been growing
have not seriously stunted its growth. In fact,
there are hundreds of other large sequoias, most
of them in relatively protected locations, in the
Sierra Nevada.

Much less protected—and much more stunted—are
the bristlecone pines (*Pinus aristata*), trees of very
high elevations. Although bristlecones grow on
mountain peaks in several western states, it is in
California and Nevada that they reach their greatest
age. One would hardly think they could survive at

all, considering the rocky, exposed, and windy slopes on which they live. As it is, they are gnarled and twisted. A tree no taller than a human being may be nearly a thousand years old. During some years the environment may be so difficult, and the trees so buried in ice and snow, that little or no growth takes place. In other years, there may be three good months of growing season. What matters is that the trees survive, and have for many centuries. One that grows in the White Mountains of California is estimated to be more than 4,600 years of age. Another in the Wheeler Peak area of Nevada is approximately 4,900 years old, and is therefore the oldest living organism.

Some trees at high altitudes endure such severe conditions that they do not produce cones or seeds. They may exist merely because they became established when winds blew seeds uphill. The trees develop as little more than shrubs. Sometimes they are nearly prostrate, hugging the ground for whatever protection it offers. This growth above tree limit is called *krummholz*, German for "crooked wood." Surprisingly, this forest—if that is what it can be called—is in places capable of providing enough protection to shelter men and beasts. A Montana outfitter, lost in a blizzard, saved his life by taking refuge in a krummholz thicket, where he was able to light a fire and stay all night while the storm raged around him.

The little willows—snow willow (*Salix nivalis*) and Arctic willow (*S. arctica*)—grow at high elevations, but they can scarcely be called shrubs, much less trees. Their world is one of freezing and thawing, and so they must be adapted to survive swift changes in soil and weather conditions. The alpine environment even has a few advantages, such as protective rocks and lee slopes where the wind's effects are not so great, and a slightly more benign climate near the ground.

On other mountain summits around the world, similar conditions are encountered, but with some striking differences. At high altitudes in tropical Africa and South America, where it is literally summer by day and winter by night, huge plants grow, much in contrast to the ground-hugging trees of similar high places in Europe and North America. On high plateaus in the Andes Mountains, well above 13,000 feet, one encounters the huge flowering stalk of *Puya raimondii*, a bromeliad in the pineapple family. Perhaps it is not really a tree, but it is certainly arborescent, for it leaps up 30 feet when it blooms, quite a spectacle amidst the nearly treeless mountains that surround it. In eastern Africa, the uplands are cold but humid, often cloaked in dense fog. On Mount Kenya and on Kilimanjaro, and the Ruwenzori mountains, among others, grow numerous species of giant groundsels (*Senecio*) and *Lobelias*. Around the Northern Hemisphere, conditions are much the same from continent to continent. Even the trees are familiar, though their species may differ. In the Alps, for example, beech forests occupy the lower slopes, mixing with spruce (*Picea abies*) at higher levels. Above that are pine (*Pinus silvestris*), larch (*Larix europaea*), and spruce. Alpine meadows host white alders (*Alnus viridis*).

The farther north we travel, the more we find mountain tundra at lower elevations. While tree line in Mexico reaches nearly to 14,000 feet, in Colorado it occurs at 11,000 feet, and in Alaska at only 3,000 feet. As in ultra-cold climates everywhere, not many trees grow unless they can find a sheltered ravine or sunny vale away from the all-destroying wind. The northernmost extent of forest in Alaska consists of black spruce (*Picea mariana*), a cylindrical tree with short needles and round cones, and white spruce (*P. glauca*), taller than the black spruce and with a more conical profile. These are not the tall and stately Sitka spruces of southern Alaska, which prosper in mild moist winds of the Pacific coast. Closer to the northern limit of trees these smaller spruces grow in a more scattered pattern, "taiga," as the Russians call it, "land of little sticks." With the ground perpetually frozen less than 2 feet beneath the moss-covered surface, the trees have little chance to put down roots that could support a trunk of large size. So the roots must spread in a lateral direction if the trees are to survive. But in doing that they are vulnerable to the heaving of the ground brought on by freezing and thawing. That tips the trees over or topples them, bothering neither the red squirrel, which scrambles about in the upper branches and nips off the cones, nor the porcupine, which eats the bark.

The spruces have other company. Where uncontrolled fires swept past in years gone by, and nearly destroyed the mature forest, quaking aspen (*Populus tremuloides*) takes over temporarily until the slow-growing spruces can recover. The balsam poplar (*P. balsamifera*), a tree that thrives throughout Canada and Alaska from the Atlantic Ocean to the Arctic, adds a fragrant aroma to the sheltered vales. Paper birches (*Betula papyrifera*) are relatively tall trees here, while the dwarf birch (*B. nana*) reaches little more than shrub height. But the dwarf birch, without so many leaves or such an area of trunk exposed, grows farther north, out across the vast treeless tundra. The far north blazes with color when fireweed (*Epilobium angustifolium*) blooms, for then the dominant hues of the taiga forest become magenta and green for as far as the eye can see.

In the Old World, the plants of Scandinavia must be adapted to withstand prolonged winters and months of weather extremes. Among the most successful are birch (*Betula*), aspen, and oak (*Quercus*). The European taiga is composed of spruce and pine forests, groves of birch, berry patches, willow thickets, and bogs.

In far northern Asia, the Siberian region has a reputation for being especially inhospitable to trees. Nevertheless, dwarf willows, birches, and other trees cling tenaciously to life in those cold expanses. Growth is slow; an old juniper on the Kola Peninsula of the U.S.S.R. measured only 3.5 inches in diameter but its growth rings indicated an age of nearly 600 years. The Siberian taiga, largest forest in the world, has a composition quite different from that of the Alaskan taiga. Instead of spruces, the principal trees are firs (*Abies sibirica*), larches (*Larix sibirica*), and pines (*Pinus cembra*). However, a spruce (*Picea excelsa*) is present; in fact, there are more types of native spruces in Asia—some 40 species—than in North America.

Life can be rich, abundant, and remarkably interconnected, wherever evolution has been perfecting the ability of plants and animals to survive the rigors of varying climates over thousands of years. There are parts of the ecological story, however, that are still obscure, notably plant distribution and animal behavior. "I often wish," said the Rocky Mountain naturalist Enos Mills some seventy years ago, "that an old beaver neighbor of mine would write the story of his life." Would that the spruce could do so, too.

201. *A lone whitebark pine* (Pinus albicaulus) *stands below Obsidian Cliff, in Yellowstone National Park. This is a tree of high mountainsides, and whitebark pines are shaped by their environment. Trees clinging to exposed locations are so constantly battered by wind that their limbs may grow only on the leeward side of the trunks. And at higher elevations, whitebark pines sprawl over the rocks, their tough limbs forming springy mats that shelter wildlife (and wilderness trekkers) during storms.* (Steven C. Wilson/ Entheos)

202 *overleaf. Exposed to fierce winds high in the Oregon Cascades, a mountain hemlock* (Tsuga mertensiana) *has lost much of its bark but clings tenaciously to life. In sheltered valleys, mountain hemlocks may tower 150 feet. But trees at timberline, as high as 11,000 feet in the Sierra Nevada, are short and gnarled, even sprawling.* (Harald Sund)

204. *Frost decorates the paired needles and cones of a lodgepole pine in the Wyoming mountains. Each scale of a cone is tipped with a curved prickle. The cones may hang on the branches for years before scattering their seeds; and the seeds may lie dormant in the forest duff for decades before they germinate.* (Thase Daniel)

205 *both. An expert climber, the mountain goat (Oreamnos americanus) spends its summers in the rocks above timberline, moving to lower elevations in winter. A North American relative of the chamois of European peaks, this stocky beast stands about 3 feet tall at its humped shoulders and may weigh 300 pounds. During*

the rut in late autumn, the billies battle one another with their sharp, backward-curved horns. (Douglas Chadwick)

206 *overleaf. Morning mist billows over an untrammeled forest in the Colorado Rockies. For most of this century, conservationists and timber interests have waged battles over proposals to set aside large areas in the American West as wilderness preserves and national parks, and over forest management practices on both public and private lands.* (Jonathan T. Wright)

205

208. *The sparsely clad spire of a subalpine fir* (Abies lasiocarpa) *is silhouetted against a dramatic sunset in the Olympic Mountains of Washington. The smallest and most widely distributed species of fir in North America, this hardy tree grows from Alaska to southern Arizona. Subalpine fir has little commercial value, but the tree plays an important ecological role in preventing soil erosion on high, steep slopes. Its seeds are vital to the diet of red squirrels.* (Harald Sund)

209. *A clump of white spruce* (Picea glauca) *provides an appropriate counterpoint to the brilliant autumn colors of the Alaskan tundra. The new needles of a white*

spruce have a pale blue or whitish tinge, which explains the tree's common name. Local people often call it the "skunk spruce" because the needles, if crushed, give off a foul odor. (Rick McIntyre)

210 *overleaf. Dwarf trees and shrubs—willow, birch, blueberry—hug the tundra along the Toklat River, in Alaska's Mount McKinley National Park. To grow prostrate here is to survive the winter gales that roar down from the Arctic. Thus a willow a century old may stand only a few inches high, though its root system spreads underground for 15 feet.* (Gary Braasch)

212. *Their true color no longer masked by green chlorophyll, the toothed leaves of dwarf birch* (Betula nana) *blaze in the Alaskan autumn. In subarctic Alaska, a truly tall birch, one growing in a sheltered location, may reach no higher than the shoulders of the moose browsing on its branches.* (Rick McIntyre)

213. *A caribou calf* (Rangifer tarandus) *sports the beginnings of antlers that, in adulthood, may span 40 inches. Though reindeer lichen are the caribou's primary food source, these big deer of the Arctic also eat willows, grasses, and herbs during their long migration treks.* (Rick McIntyre)

214 *overleaf. Nearly one-tenth of the flowering plants on Earth belong to the tremendous composite, or daisy, family. Of those 20,000 species, one of the strangest is the giant groundsel* (Senecio keniodendron) *found on the misty heights of East African mountains.* (M. Philip Kahl/N.A.S./Photo Researchers, Inc.)

lets contain chlorophyll and function just like leaves, for the actual foliage of these unusual trees has been reduced to tiny scales. Most species in the genus Schefflera are epiphytic shrubs and trees with evergreen leaves. One of those reaching tree size, with a height of 80 feet, is Schefflera volkensii of East Africa; another is the Queensland umbrella tree widely grown as a houseplant, or in the tropics as a landscape tree. (Hans D. Dossenbach)

218 overleaf. At 14,000 feet in the Peruvian Andes, a relict forest of quishuar trees (Buddleia coriacea) survives in a reserve set aside for vicunas. This tree belongs to the logania family, notorious for deadly poisons such as strychnine. The genus Buddleia includes many warm-climate trees and shrubs that have showy yellow or lilac flowers, among them the butterfly bush of China. (Francois Gohier)

216. Though it suggests a huge cabbage set atop a palm trunk that may be 20 feet tall, the flowers of the giant groundsel are unquestionably those of a member of the daisy clan. This groundsel forest was photographed at 13,000 feet on Mount Kenya. (M. Philip Kahl/ N.A.S./Photo Researchers, Inc.)

217. Lichens clothe a stand of casuarinas on the highlands of Mount Kenya, in East Africa. Flanking trees with large, palmate leaves represent the genus Schefflera. Most of the 45 species in the genus Casuarina are found in Australia, and commonly are called "Australian pines" because their slender branchlets resemble pine needles. Indeed, the branch-

220. *Tamaracks and larches are unusual members of the large conifer clan. Most conifers are evergreen but trees in the genus* Larix *are among the few that shed their foliage annually. Rarest of the group in North America is the subalpine larch* (Larix lyalli) *found at timberline in rugged, isolated mountains—but only in widely scattered areas of Washington, Idaho, Montana, British Columbia, and Alberta. Anchored in scant soil by a powerful root system, the subalpine larch is unfazed by gale winds and heavy burdens of snow in winter. An ancient tree, one 5 centuries old, may stand only 30 feet high; but it has its moment of great glory in September, when its needles turn a luminous gold against vivid blue skies.* (Harald Sund)

221. *Near timberline in the Alpine Lakes region of Washington, a Sitka mountain ash* (Sorbus sitchensis) *clings to a crevice at the foot of a great granite boulder. First discovered near Sitka, Alaska, this shrub produces masses of bright red berries that are devoured by grouse and thrushes.* (Harald Sund)

222 *overleaf. The glacial boulder and Jeffrey pine* (Pinus jeffreyi) *atop a dome in Yosemite National Park would appear to have been set in position by a sculptor. A mountain tree that grows from southern Oregon to Baja California, Jeffrey pine has a huge cone, up to 15 inches long, that suggests a beehive.* (M. P. L. Fogden)

224 *and* **225.** *Sculpted by a harsh environment where few other trees could survive, the wood of bristlecone pines* (Pinus aristata) *atop the White Mountains of California is an inexhaustible photographic subject. These are the oldest living things on Earth: bristlecone pines live for 3,000 to 5,000 years at elevations as high as 11,000 feet. The tree's name is self-explanatory: its cone scales are tipped with long, thin bristles.*

Bristlecone pines are found on limestone or dolomite soils above an elevation of 5,500 feet. Botanists recently divided the group into two species. The Great Basin bristlecone pine (P. longaeva) *is found in Utah, Nevada, and western California; the Rocky Mountain bristlecone pine* (P. aristata) *is native to the peaks of Colorado, New Mexico, and Arizona. Though relatively soft and brittle, the wood of bristlecone pines once was used to support mine shafts. The seeds from its cones are eaten by the relatively few birds found at high*

altitudes: Clark's nutcracker,
Townsend's solitaire, and the
white-crowned sparrow. (224 all
and 225 left Richard Rowan; *225*
center and right David Muench)

226 *overleaf. Bristlecone pines*
(Pinus aristata) *growing below*
treeline become handsome, many-
branched trees. But those exposed
to raging storms on barren
mountaintops, where snow falls
year-round, are gnarled and
twisted, often with only strips of
bark still attached to the trunk.
(Betty Randall)

230 *overleaf. Sunset over Sequoia National Park. The soft, light wood of giant sequoias was in demand for shingles, timbers, and casks, and the groves were ravaged by 19th century lumbermen until the U.S. Congress took action in time to save some of the finest remaining trees. But the greatest sequoias of all were lost to the saw. The annual growth rings of one stump exceeded 4,000, and one tree felled for the mill was estimated to be 400 feet tall.* (M. P. L. Fogden)

228 *and* **229.** *The largest living thing on Earth, and among the oldest, is the giant sequoia* (Sequoiadendron giganteum) *of California. Groves of sequoias grow on the western slopes of the Sierra Nevada, and the largest of their kind—the General Sherman Tree, named for the Civil War hero— is 295 feet tall and 36½ feet in diameter at its base. A typical sequoia may live for 3,000 years and weigh 2,000 tons.* (228 Harald Sund; 229 Steven C. Wilson/ Entheos)

232. *Mohave yuccas* (Yucca schidigera) *are in full flower in the desert of southeastern California. Some 40 species of yuccas are found in North America, 11 of them growing tall enough to be considered trees. Mohave yucca, with evergreen bayonet leaves 2 feet long, attains a height of 20 feet. Its large, creamy-white flowers are packed into a cluster 2½ feet tall. The yucca leaves, which persist for several years, are used to make baskets, mats, and rope.*
(David Muench)

Dry Forests:
Trees of Arid Lands

The question is not why prickly pear cactuses grow on the equator but why they reach tree size in the Galápagos Islands. Not because of abundant water; the islands are arid. And not because of hot weather. The Galápagos Archipelago, 600 miles off the west coast of South America, is so cool that fur seals and penguins live there. Owing to the Humboldt Current, which flows north from Antarctica, the islands are laved with cool water, cool air, and cool fog. It is no small wonder that a cactus even gets started, much less reaches tree size.

Yet on Santa Cruz Island grows one of the world's most puzzling forests. It is composed of the familiar prickly pear, but there the species grows to 40 feet tall, with some trees attaining a trunk more than 3 feet in diameter. A visitor feels as though he were back in a North American ponderosa pine forest: the trunks have a furrowed bark of orange plates. There seems no reason why this prickly pear (*Opuntia echios* var. *giganteum*) should attain tree form. *Opuntias*, which grow naturally in virtually every arid environment in the Western Hemisphere, are usually prostrate or sprawling. They may grow in good-sized clumps, but in few places elsewhere do they develop into trees. Their familiar round pads, one growing out of another, succulent, green, bristling with inch-long spines, make them a desert trademark. Many birds nest in them; the spines provide excellent protection against marauding predators.

Huge cactuses aren't exceptional in arid lands. *Jasminocereus*, normally a tree-sized cactus, grows in the Galápagos Islands. The saguaro (*Cereus*

giganteus) of arid North America reaches
50 feet in height and may weigh more than
10 tons.

The prickly pear simply keeps what little moisture
it gets and stores it for long periods. Its pads
swell when rain falls, then shrivel and wrinkle
during periods of prolonged drought. The cardons
(*Pachycereus*) of Mexico, largest of cactuses—up
to 60 feet tall—seem obedient to the same survival
plan. But getting and keeping water is by no means
limited to members of the cactus family. *Euphorbias*
in such locales as the arid Canary Islands, off the
African coast, have grown to tree size and have
succulent arms.

Extreme heat is another challenge. Sometimes desert
trees must endure temperatures that would be
excruciating to man. At the seedling stage they live
near the ground surface, where, in a typical desert
on a typical hot day, the temperature may be 180°F.
in the shade. Animals may avoid such temperatures,
but trees cannot. Cactuses have actually been frost-
bitten during winter extremes when snow fell and icy
winds turned the succulent green trunks to dying
masses of black pulp.

Floods and high winds provide additional dangers.
Particles of sand blown along the ground for days
can literally saw and undercut a sturdy tree until it
is beyond the threshold of survival.

For the most part, these attacks are warded off by
ingenious methods of resistance. Cactuses have tough
pads and stems that restrict any evaporation that
might waste precious moisture. Some trees such as
cottonwoods (*Populus*) and salt cedar (*Tamarix*) keep
to streams or springs where their roots can reach
dependable moisture supplies. Few trees of arid
lands take more immediate advantage of rainfall
than the ocotillo (*Fouquieria splendens*), which
normally resembles a bundle of whiplashes but
bursts into leaf shortly after a good rain. When
drought returns, the leaves wither and fall and the
plant looks dead once more. In the Galápagos Islands,
the widespread palo santo tree (*Bursera graveolens*)
loses its leaves during the dry season. Paloverdes
(*Cercidium*) manufacture chlorophyll in their green
trunks and stems. In certain cactuses, such as the
prickly pear, the leaves have been reduced to spines.
As any desert devotee can testify, arid woods are
full of thorns, spikes, and hooks. We would not care

to rush blindly into a thicket of mesquite (*Prosopis juliflora*), a member of the legume family.

Nor is there much intimate fraternizing with another legume, the *Acacia*, a genus of trees more associated with arid and semiarid lands than with any other environment. Acacias grow in virtually every desert in the world. Most have thorns—some curved like cat's claws, some stout and as straight as stilettos, but all apparently designed to fend off animal attack. Acacias have thrived through millennia of evolution in association with animals. The camel thorn (*Acacia giraffe*) and umbrella thorn (*A. tortilis*) are familiar trees that spread over the drier parts of eastern and southern Africa. One secret of its success is that the acacia's feathery foliage prevents damaging exposure to drying winds. Many desert plants send roots as deep as 80 feet to tap what underground moisture there is. Gum arabic (*A. nilotica*) covers parts of Africa, Europe, and Asia. If it doesn't rain in parts of South Africa for years, the sweet thorn (*A. karroo*) puts out no leaves for years. Such slow-growth success stories are common among acacias. Some master the environment so well that they reach 90 feet in height. Or in bloom they resemble a shower of golden coins, such as numerous Australian wattles, with their cascades of yellow stamens. These often mix with eucalypts and provide a breathtaking explosion of yellow in early spring—especially the golden wattles, which include *A. longifolia*, *A. pycnantha*, and *A. saligna*.

But we have not solved the riddle of the Galápagos. Arborescent prickly pears have adaptations similar to those of other desert trees. They lack normal leaves; hence they conserve moisture. Their spines ward off attack by wild animals. Or do they? We pause a moment to ponder what wildlife attacks these cactuses. Marine iguanas subsist on marine plants. Finches use the cactuses as perches, or wield a cactus spine as a tool with which to dig insects out of holes. The culprit could be the giant tortoise, but this reptile is not such a giant that it can climb up into the cactus to reach the succulent pads. At the same time, tortoises *do* eat pads. For when rain falls, pads on the plants fill out and grow heavy with moisture; after a time they break off and fall from the ends of the branches to the forest floor. We have watched the tortoises eating them with gusto, or what seems like gusto. That still doesn't explain why a normally small cactus should grow into trees. But it is true that tortoises relish cactus, and perhaps that is the key we are seeking.

A long time ago, according to one theory, the prickly pears, usually low-growing, arrived in the Galápagos Islands. Then the tortoises arrived and began to eat prickly pear pads, the only source of fresh water in a land of lava where moisture sinks into the earth and disappears. As time went on vigorous cactuses that raised their pads up beyond the reach of tortoises survived and reproduced. They grew taller as the generations passed, literally adapting to escape the hungry tortoises. Any cactuses growing on cliffs where tortoises couldn't get at them produced seeds that kept the species replenished. Seedlings might have been vulnerable to tortoises were they not enveloped in abundant spines and after a few growing seasons thrust their succulent pads up out of reach. By the time the plant matures it drops its basal spines and acquires a tough thick bark that the tortoise cannot penetrate. Spines on upper branches, not needed for protection against tortoises, have evolved into soft bristles.

If all this really happened as the evidence suggests, then it is a notable example of a tree adapting to an animal. Perhaps this theory is a bit too simplistic and we should be skeptical. But then we shouldn't be surprised, either. Dry-land trees worldwide exhibit remarkable adaptations to their environments. Alas, however, the desert can't always cope with an animal as vigorous and ubiquitous and destructive as man. The lowering of water tables over large areas, for example, has taken moisture away from roots and eradicated desert vegetation. Man has also made deserts by cutting the trees originally there. Such destruction occurred for thousands of years in what is now Turkey, but the love of forests never quite died. Kemal Atatürk, widely revered president of Turkey from 1923 until his death in 1938, once said: "Eyes that may not look on greenery are deprived of the pleasure that verdure alone can give. Reforest this place so abundantly that even a blind person may at least feel the wealth of trees around him."

237. *An ancient saguaro cactus* (Cereus giganteus), *perhaps three centuries old, at Organ Pipe Cactus National Monument in Arizona. The demand for cacti for collections and landscaping has caused many desert areas to be stripped of their prickly native flora by lawless cactus rustlers. Many of the 250 species of cactus in North America are now considered to be threatened with extinction.* (Steven C. Wilson/Entheos)

238. *The accordion-pleat structure of a saguaro's trunk and arms enables the giant cactus to expand and contract, depending on the moisture supply. But in heavy rains, the cactus may burst open if its roots take up more water than the succulent cells are able to store.* (Betty Randall)

239 *top left. An adult cactus wren* (Campylorhynchus brunneicapillus) *feasts on the scarlet, figlike fruit of a saguaro. Some 2,000 shiny black seeds pepper the pulp of each saguaro fruit; the seeds feed desert birds, rodents, and insects such as harvester ants. A cactus forest may be populated by 15 to 20 saguaros per acre, and together they will produce ten million seeds over a five-year span. But during that period only a single saguaro seedling is likely to establish itself.* (Jen and Des Bartlett/ Bruce Coleman, Inc.)

239 *top right. Waxy white flowers bloom in spring at the tips of a saguaro's trunk and main branches. Only a third of the buds will open; many are damaged by beetle larvae and by birds attracted by the insect infestation. Saguaro flowers open at night and close the following afternoon; longnose bats, feeding on their nectar, are the major pollinator.* (Steven C. Wilson/ Entheos)

239 *above. The smallest owl in North America, no larger than a sparrow, an elf owl* (Micrathene whitneyi) *peers from its nest cavity in an old saguaro. At least 16 species of birds use football-shaped cavities originally chiseled in saguaros by woodpeckers and flickers. The nest holes are hollowed out months ahead of the nesting season to allow the cactus time to seal off the wound with a wall of woody tissue a half-inch thick.* (Des Bartlett/Bruce Coleman, Ltd.)

240 *overleaf. Of the 2,000 plants in the genus* Euphorbia, Cooper's *spurge* (Euphorbia cooperi) *is one of a handful of species that reach tree size in the deserts of South Africa. Though these* euphorbias *resemble cacti, with fleshy green branches that function as leaves, they have a milky sap and their spines, where they occur, are solitary or in pairs. In South Africa tree-size* euphorbias *are commonly called "nabooms."* (Walter H. Hodge)

242. *Largest native palm in the continental United States, the desert palm* (Washingtonia filifera) *is named for George Washington, first President of the United States. This rare palm, which grows to a height of 50 feet, is restricted to a small range in the deserts of Arizona, California, and Baja California. It is sometimes called the "petticoat palm" because of the persistant dead leaves that hang against the gigantic trunk. This palm is now planted in tropical and subtropical gardens around the world.* (Walter H. Hodge)

243. *Except for one species, plants in the mistletoe family (Loranthaceae) are mostly small parasites that get food and water from the tissues of their unfortunate host trees. The exception is the 30-foot-tall "Christmas tree"* (Nuytsia floribunda) *of western Australia deserts. Adorned with clusters of bright orange flowers, this tree mistletoe has green leaves capable of photosynthesis, although some botanists believe the plant may also parasitize the root systems of desert grasses.* (Walter H. Hodge)

244 *above. A member of the Agave family, the Joshua tree (*Yucca brevifolia*) inhabits the sun-scored mesas of Utah and Arizona. Its leaves, clustered at the tips of thick branches, are evergreen bayonets 6 to 10 inches long and armed along the blade with countless tiny, sharp teeth.* (Tom Meyers)

244 *above. Dense gray hairs that cover the young branches give the smoke tree (*Dalea spinosa*) the appearance of a puff of smoke when the tree is seen from a distance. To prevent the loss of moisture in the harsh environment of a desert wash, the smoke tree is leafless most of the year. Purple flowers that appear briefly in spring produce hard-shelled seeds that germinate only when they are broken open by being tumbled against rocks in a sudden flood.* (Betty Randall)

245. *Though the pear-shaped fruits of jumping cholla (*Opuntia fulgida*) produce prodigious amounts of seed, this small tree cactus of the Sonoran Desert rarely reproduces in normal fashion. Rather, its joints are easily knocked loose—and quickly take root where they fall, sometimes after hitchhiking on the back of a wild animal.* (Jeff Foott)

246 *overleaf. Though eventually it may be buried alive by shifting sands, a Utah juniper (*Juniperus osteosperma*) thrives for the present amidst the dunes of Arizona's Monument Valley. It has, after all, survived for several centuries under conditions that long ago would have claimed trees of lesser stamina. Once gathered as food by Indians, the sweet berry-like cones of Utah juniper today are left for wildlife. And deer browse its foliage.* (Harald Sund)

250 *overleaf. The tree that South Africans call the kokerboom* (Aloe dichotoma) *belongs to the lily family. Attaining a height of 30 feet, it forms an open "forest" in dry, rocky areas. The kokerboom leaves are succulent, and its flowers are so full of nectar that they attract not only insects and birds but sweet-toothed baboons. The "wood" is light and fibrous but strong enough to support a huge crown of water-filled branches plus the massive nests of weaver finches.* (Klaus Paysan)

248 *and* **249.** *In the Galápagos Islands, prickly-pear cacti* (Opuntia sp.) *have evolved into trees as tall as 40 feet, with thick bark that is a defense against browsing tortoises. And young opuntia trees have additional armor—dense, stiff, and very sharp spines that are eventually shed as the tree grows. Tortoises and land iguanas eat the juicy cactus pads, ignoring their whorls of spines. And cactus finches feed on the bright flowers.* (David Cavagnaro)

254 *overleaf. Squatting on its massive trunk, the elephant tree* (Bursera microphylla) *is an uncommon tree of rocky desert slopes in Arizona, California, and Mexico. Not much is known about its natural history; indeed, it was not until 1937 that the first elephant trees were discovered growing in the United States. An old specimen that has attained a height of 16 feet will have branches that spread 30 to 40 feet. The elephant tree yields aromatic oil and a resinous gum that is used in Mexico as a varnish and glue.* (David Muench)

252 *both. Tamarisks* (Tamarix sp.) *scattered over the North African desert represent a hardy group of trees and shrubs that can thrive in the hottest weather and poorest soils, even on alkali flats and saline shores. Their featherlike foliage is designed to conserve scarce moisture. Native to Eurasia and Africa, tamarisks often are planted as ornamentals and wind-breaks and have colonized desert watercourses in the southwestern United States.* (Klaus Paysan)

253. *A euphorbia survives in the stony Cameroon desert of West Africa. The milky latex of some species of Euphorbia, like* Euphorbia intisy *of Madagascar, is rich in rubber, and has had some local use; however, it cannot compete commercially with* hevea *rubber. Like some cacti, tree euphorbias can expand or shrink their fleshy branches—depending on the water supply.* (Peter Ward/Bruce Coleman, Ltd.)

Notes on Photographers

Jen and Des Bartlett (239 top left, 239 bottom), a well-known husband-and-wife team of wildlife photographers, recently won an Emmy Award for their outstanding *World of Survival* television series.

Wolfgang Bayer (40) is a wildlife film producer who has made television films for the National Geographic Society, Walt Disney Productions and *Wild Wild World of Animals*.

Gary Braash (119 right, 128 overleaf, 210 overleaf), a freelance photographer living in Vancouver, Washington, specializes in landscape photography. His nature photographs have appeared in numerous magazines, calendars, and Time-Life Books.

Jim Brandenburg (127 top, 156 top, 192, 193), a native Minnesotan, is a contract photographer for *National Geographic*. He has contributed to numerous articles and books and recently photographed North American animals for a set of postage stamps.

Stanley Breeden (38 overleaf, 58 bottom, 142 bottom left, 142 bottom right, 145 bottom) is an Australian photographer whose work has appeared in *National Geographic, Audubon* and many books.

Richard W. Brown (162, 163 bottom, 170 overleaf, 180, 181) lives on a Vermont farm and is currently working on his own book, *The Last of the Hill Farms*. He has photographed rural subjects from New England to New Zealand. His work has appeared in *National Wildlife* and *Audubon*.

Fred Bruemmer (190 overleaf) was a newspaper photographer and reporter in Canada before becoming a specialist in Arctic wildlife. He has written hundreds of articles and several books, including *The Life of the Harp Seal*. His photographs have appeared in many books, including *The Audubon Society Book of Marine Wildlife*.

Sonja Bullaty and Angelo Lomeo (68, 83, 85, 88, 160 overleaf, 163 top right) are a husband-and-wife team whose picture essays have appeared in *Life, Horizon,* and various nature books, including *The Audubon Society Field Guide to North American Trees* (two volumes). She was born in Prague, Czechoslovakia, he in New York.

R. I. M. Campbell (54 overleaf) is a British nature photographer living in Nairobi, Kenya. He has produced a number of films for the "World of Survival" television series.

James H. Carmichael, Jr. (25) teaches nature photography in Sarasota, Florida. His wildlife pictures have been published in many books and magazines such as *National Geographic* and *National Wildlife*.

Robert P. Carr (168, 174 overleaf), who spent his early years "chasing animals and climbing trees" in Michigan, turned to photography as a profession so he could pursue his lifelong interest in wildlife and natural subjects. His work has appeared in many books and magazines.

Stewart Cassidy (56) specializes in international wildlife subjects and has traveled extensively. His photographs have appeared in numerous magazines and in National Geographic books.

Patricia Caulfield (84) is a Manhattan-based freelance photographer who specializes in natural history. She has contributed to many magazines and books including *The Audubon Society Book of Wildflowers*.

David Cavagnaro (248, 249 left, 249 right) studied entomology in California. This led, in 1961, to participation in an entomological expedition to Southeast Asia and Australia. He now lives in California.

Douglas Chadwick (205 top, 205 bottom) spent 7 years studying mountain goats in Montana's Rocky Mountains. His photographs of goats and other animals have appeared in numerous magazines including *Sports Illustrated, Country Journal* and *National Geographic*.

Joseph T. Collins (45), a member of the staff of the University of Kansas, at Lawrence, is an herpetologist and teaches natural history.

Ed Cooper (184) is a native New Yorker whose love of nature led him to the Pacific Northwest, where he has worked as a professional photographer since 1968.

Thase Daniel (204), a resident of Arkansas, first taught music but now devotes herself to photographing wildlife in remote parts of many countries. She has contributed to many wildlife magazines and books.

Harold Davis (177) is primarily a landscape photographer. His work has appeared in numerous publications and is represented in the permanent collections of the Bank of America and the Museum of the City of New York.

Nicholas F. Delagi (159 bottom) is a retired criminal court judge who photographs wildlife in the United States. His work has been published in *Funk and Wagnall's New Encyclopedia* and in Sierra Club calendars.

Jack Dermid (158, 159 top), a widely known nature photographer, lives in Wilmington, North Carolina. He is co-author of *The World of the Wood Duck* and has completed a film entitled *The Living Coast*.

Stephanie Dinkins (104) is a nature photographer who is a native of Louisiana and has traveled extensively in Africa and Asia.

Hans D. Dossenbach (26, 57 left, 217) was born in Switzerland and studied animal behavior in Vienna and photography in Zurich. He is the author and photographer of many books, including *The Family Life of Birds*.

John Eastcott and Yva Momatiuk (79 top, 79 bottom, 80 overleaf, 172 bottom, 173), a well-known husband-and-wife team, regularly undertake photographic assignments in the wilderness areas of the world. Their work has appeared in a number of books, including *The Wild Places*, *Wild Shores of North America* and a book on New Zealand's High Country.

Jean-Paul Ferrero (141) is a wildlife photographer whose work has been published in many international publications and books, including *The Audubon Society Book of Wild Animals* and *The Audubon Society Book of Marine Wildlife*.

Michael P. L. Fogden (222 overleaf, 230 overleaf) is a professional biologist with a doctorate in ornithology from Oxford University. He has spent the past 15 years researching wildlife in Borneo, Uganda and Mexico. His photographs have appeared in many books and magazines, and he is co-author (with his wife) of *Animals and Their Colours*.

Alan Foley (146 overleaf) is a wildlife photographer and heads his own photograph agency in Australia.

Jeffrey O. Foott (245), a marine biologist and photographer, has filmed wildlife programs for Survival Anglia, a film production company associated with the World Wildlife Fund. His work has been reproduced in such magazines as *Audubon* and *National Geographic*, as well as in many books.

François Gohier (64, 218 overleaf) is a freelance writer and photographer specializing in South American subjects. His articles and photographs have appeared in many publications, including *The Audubon Society Book of Marine Wildlife*.

Su Gooders (154 overleaf) directs the British wildlife photograph agency Ardea in London.

Keith Gunnar (123), primarily a wilderness photographer, illustrated *Backpacking, One Step at a Time*. Living in Washington, he concentrates on "self-propelled" outdoor activities such as canoeing, hiking and skiing, in the Pacific Northwest.

Robert C. Hermes (41 top right) is one of the early members of the National Audubon Society. He has covered the entire natural history field in motion pictures and stills. Living in Homestead, Florida, he is interested in painting as well as photography.

Robert Hernandez (98 overleaf), a specialist in environmental studies, is a cruise director on the Lindblad vessel, *Explorer*. He also serves as an assistant to the Survival Anglia television unit, a film company associated with the World Wildlife Fund.

Walter H. Hodge (16, 28 overleaf, 30, 31, 34, 35, 65 right, 113, 114, 115, 136, 143, 144, 145 top, 164 bottom, 240 overleaf, 242, 243), the co-author of *The Audubon Society Book of Wildflowers*, is a leading American botanist. A photographer of natural history throughout the world, he has written nearly 200 papers on botany, horticulture and general natural history.

M. Philip Kahl (214 overleaf, 216), who holds a doctorate in zoology, is a wildlife photographer and ecology consultant living in Naples, Florida. Most recently he has studied storks and flamingos of the world. His work has been published in many natural history magazines.

Stephen J. Krasemann (120 overleaf, 130 bottom right), a Wisconsin-based photographer, is a regular contributor to many books and magazines, among them *National Geographic* and *Natural History.*

Tom and Pat Leeson (126) specialize in photographing nature in the Pacific Northwest. They have contributed to National Geographic books, and various magazines such as *Natural History* and *Audubon.*

Sven-Olaf Lindblad (62 overleaf), born in Sweden, now lives in the United States. He has photographed nature throughout the world, particularly in East Africa, the Arctic and Antarctica.

Susan McCartney (66 overleaf), a travel photographer, has just completed an assignment for *Realités* magazine. Before becoming a photographer, she studied fine art and graphic design.

Lynn McClaren (60 overleaf) lived and photographed in East Africa for many years. Now residing in Boston, she is currently interested in photographing medical subjects.

Tom McHugh (41 top left) is a professional cinematographer who did his first work for Walt Disney Productions. In recent years he has specialized in nature photography.

Loren McIntyre (37 top and bottom, 41 bottom, 46 overleaf) is a professional writer and photographer specializing in South American subjects. His work has appeared in *National Geographic,* Time-Life books, and *Wildlife of the Forests,* among others.

Rick McIntyre (209, 212, 213) is a naturalist working with the park services at Mt. McKinley National Park and Death Valley. He has supplied articles and photographs for *Alaska* magazine and a children's book, *Denali National Park,* as well as National Geographic books.

Wendell D. Metzen (78, 82) is a biologist-photographer who lives in Florida. His wildlife photographs have been reproduced in *National Geographic, National Wildlife* and Time-Life books.

Tony Morrison (65 left), a zoologist who has specialized in South American subjects for 20 years, has written for Time-Life books and produced documentary films for the BBC. In America his work has appeared in Time-Life books and *National Geographic.*

David Muench (73, 90 overleaf, 106 overleaf, 196, 225 middle and right, 232, 254 overleaf) is a widely acclaimed photographer who specializes in photographing the western landscape. Among his many book credits are *California* (with Ray Atkeson), *Arizona* and *Desert Images: An American Landscape* (with Edward Abbey).

Tom Myers (244 left), a natural history photographer living in Sacramento, California, has had photographs published in *National Geographic* and in many books, including *The Wild Shores of North America.*

Thomas Nebbia's (58 top) photographic career began when he was an Army combat cameraman during the Korean War. He has freelanced for *National Geographic,* and his prizewinning work has appeared in *The Audubon Society Book of Wild Animals,* among other books.

David Overcash (164 top left), an electrician by trade, has been a professional photographer for 18 years. His work has illustrated textbooks, calendars, billboards, TV logos and magazine covers, including the *New York Times Magazine.*

Klaus Paysan (53, 250 overleaf, 252 both) is an award winning German wildlife photographer who also heads a picture agency.

Carroll W. Perkins (178 overleaf), a Canadian chemist who prefers to be known as a photographer, has had his photographs included in *Reader's Digest* and *Butterflies of the World.* His work appears regularly in Canadian publications such as *Ontario Naturalist* and *Nature Canada.*

D. C. H. Plowes (57 right), a resident of Zimbabwe, specializes in nature photography. The plant *Aloe plowessi* was discovered by him in 1950 and was named in his honor. His work appears in *The Audubon Society Book of Wildflowers* and in many publications worldwide.

Betty Randall (226 overleaf, 238, 244 right) became a career photographer after 20 years of work in medical laboratory research. Her pictures, primarily of deserts, mountains and the shores of the western United States, have appeared in several books and in *Audubon.*

Edward S. Ross (22 overleaf, 59), curator of insects at the California Academy of Sciences, was a pioneer in candid insect photography, with his *Insects Close Up.* He has photographed nature in almost every part of the globe and his work appears in hundreds of publications.

Richard Rowan (172 top, 224 all and 225 left) is a professional photographer who specializes in natural history subjects. He lives on the Monterey Peninsula, and travels world-wide.

Joe Rychetnik (194 overleaf) photographed Alaska during his residence there. He now lives in the San Francisco area.

Kjell B. Sandved (24, 36, 48, 108, 142 top left, 142 top right) produces films in association with biologists at the Museum of Natural History of the Smithsonian Institution. He also lectures on animal behavior throughout the country for the Smithsonian Associates.

John Shaw (cover, 6 overleaf, 21, 27, 32 overleaf, 44, 75, 76 overleaf, 89, 164 top right, 165, 166 overleaf, 169, 176, 182 overleaf) is a professional photographer living in Harrison, Michigan. His photographs have appeared in magazines such as *Natural Wildlife* and *Audubon* and in numerous books, filmstrips, texts and advertisements.

Caulion Singletary (101, 102 overleaf) has a printing business in Homestead, Florida, but photographing nature, and especially birds, has long been his major interest. His work has appeared in major nature publications, among them *The Wild Places.*

Charles Steinhacker (4 overleaf) is director of Nature Photography of America. His books include *Yellowstone: A Century of the Wilderness Idea* and *The Sand County of Aldo Leopold,* and he contributed to *The Wilderness Rivers of North America.*

Harald Sund (2 overleaf, 86 overleaf, 105, 118, 124 overleaf, 132, 133, 134 overleaf, 202 overleaf, 208, 220, 221, 228, 246 overleaf) lives in Washington and spends much of his time photographing the Pacific Coast and western mountains. His work has appeared in many national publications and books, including *The Wild Shores of North America.*

James P. Valentine (1, 74, 92, 97, 163 top left) is a native of Highlands, North Carolina, where he has established a conservation center, the Quest Foundation. His work has appeared in several books, including *The Wild Places.*

Kees van den Berg (148) is a Dutchman who loves to photograph his country in all seasons.

John de Visser (153) became a photographer after moving to Canada from the Netherlands in 1952. His work appears in more than 100 books, including *The Wild Shores of North America.*

Peter Ward (253) was a British nature photographer and ecologist, with a special interest in desert life.

Larry West (157) is a professional nature photographer whose photographs can be seen in many magazines and books, including *The Wild Places, The Audubon Society Book of Wild Animals,* and *The Audubon Society Book of Wildflowers.*

Steven C. Wilson (14 overleaf, 100, 116 overleaf, 119 left, 122, 127 bottom, 130 top, 130 bottom left, 131, 189, 201, 229, 237, 239 top right) studied fisheries at the University of Washington, photography at Los Angeles Art Center, and is now a director of the ENTHEOS group. His most recent project is his book, *A Natural Collection.*

Belinda Wright (42 top, 42 bottom, 43) lives in India. She has co-produced a series of wildlife films for Time-Life, and her pictures have appeared in many publications, including *National Geographic.*

Jonathan T. Wright (156 bottom, 206 overleaf), a mountaineer from Aspen, Colorado, had work published in *Natural History, National Geographic* and *National Wildlife.*

Index

Numbers in italics indicate pictures

263